The
BLANCHE SAUNDERS'
OBEDIENCE
TRAINING COURSES

NOVICE * OPEN * UTILITY * TRACKING

by

BLANCHE SAUNDERS

Illustrated by Gloria Strang

NEW COMBINED EDITION
Second Printing—1977

HOWELL BOOK HOUSE Inc.
730 Fifth Avenue, New York, N. Y. 10019

BOOK ONE

NOVICE

OBEDIENCE COURSE

CONTENTS FOR BOOK ONE
NOVICE OBEDIENCE COURSE

THE DOG FOR YOU

Owning the right dog is a pleasure. Owning the wrong one presents problems. If buying a dog is a new experience, before you buy, attend dog shows and talk with exhibitors. Ask about coat care and which breeds require professional clipping and trimming.

Talk with dog handlers and trainers. They work with all types of dogs and can tell you the breeds that are gentle and those that are more difficult to train. Discuss dogs with people who raise them, but don't expect an unbiased opinion. Kennel owners have their favorite breeds. Read books, magazines and dog publications. You will learn a lot through reading. Consult the "Selection Guide" in this book.

There are other ways you can learn about dogs. Inquire of your local Kennel Club about Puppy and Sanctioned Matches. Attend as a spectator. Talk with the neighborhood veterinarian. Most veterinarians are willing to answer "doggie" questions. Visit nearby kennels, but telephone first. Kennel owners have a busy schedule. Inquire at your local pet shops about free booklets that will tell you about dogs. Finally, ask those persons who already have a dog where they got theirs and what they like or dislike about their particular breed.

BUYING THE DOG

When it comes to buying the dog, The American Kennel Club, 51 Madison Ave., New York, N.Y., the national organization that specializes in purebred dogs, can advise you. Dogs are not kept on the premises, but the AKC, as it is called, will tell you about kennel owners and dog breeders.

Some dog clubs specialize in a single breed. If you are interested in one special kind of dog, write to the club secretary. You can find the name and address in dog magazines or dog show catalogs. The name and address will also be on record at The American Kennel Club.

A purebred dog may cost $100 or more, depending upon the popularity of the breed. Before buying a puppy, study the Standard for the breed so you will recognize good and bad features. For instance, two-colored Poodles are not accepted in the show ring. Neither are Boxers with too much white. Some breeds have to be a certain size. The Standard for **every** breed recognized in the United States is given in **The Complete Dog Book,** published by The American Kennel Club.

Before you decide on a puppy, visit different kennels. You may feel yourself drawn to one puppy more than another. While looking, don't expect to handle every puppy you see. Germs are easily carried from one kennel to another. Owners have to be cautious.

If you leave home with definite plans to get a dog, carry newspapers and towels for the return trip. Most puppies get carsick, although when you take a puppy riding every day, he should get used to the rock and roll of a motor car.

Take along a collar and leash. Nothing fancy. Just something that will get your puppy home safely if he is too big to hold in your arms.

Will it be a boy dog or a girl dog? The gentle, easy-to-handle female will cause inconvenience by coming in season but this can be overcome through spaying. Before you spay, let her develop, both mentally and physically. Spaying is usually done after six months of age and before the bitch comes in season the first time. (Remember that if you have the bitch spayed, she will be disqualified for competition in the breed ring.) If you want a dog with a more daring spirit, get a male, although males are apt to roam more and you have to watch their house manners. Where other dogs are concerned, males sometimes wear a chip on their shoulder, but either sex make good pets and good companions.

Think about age. The younger the puppy, the more quickly he will adjust to a new home. A six- or eight-weeks-old puppy requires extra care but when a puppy gets used to loud noises and unexpected situations early in life, he grows up a calmer adult dog.

Whether you buy from a kennel, from a pet shop, or from a private breeder (one who breeds his one or two pet dogs), ask questions:

Is the dog registered or eligible for registration with The American Kennel Club? You might want to breed, or to exhibit at dog shows.

What about inoculations? Write down the names of the shots that were given.

Ask when the puppy was last wormed and the kind of worms he had, if any.

Take note of health and general appearance. A healthy puppy will be active and full of play. His eyes will be bright and his coat shiny.

A puppy that cringes in the corner, is afraid of loud noises, and runs from people, is a shy puppy. Don't buy him. Shyness is hard to overcome.

All puppies are cute, but they don't stay puppies. Ask to see the parents so you will have some idea of what the puppy will look like when grown.

Ask what the puppy has been eating so you won't have to change his diet suddenly.

Request a copy of the puppy's pedigree through four generations, and, since some dogs change color when they mature, ask about a possible color change.

The final act will be the signing of the transfer slip or a paper for individual registration with The American Kennel Club.

BLANCHE SAUNDERS'
SELECTION GUIDE FOR DOG BREEDS

Successful training depends upon the breed, the age and the temperament of the dog, which is one way of saying that every dog can be trained, but certain factors, physical and otherwise, influence the ease of training and determine how pleasant a dog can be to live with.

Very small breeds, because of their size, seldom present a training problem. Even the most determined character is easily handled and can be made to obey. Small dogs can be yappier than large dogs; they can be quicker to nip and they do not hesitate to leave their calling card when they want to assert their authority. Small dogs appear to live longer.

Terrier breeds are characterized by their gameness and pep. Cocky and sure of themselves, with the instinct to unearth anything that moves, Terrier breeds make active, energetic companions. Eager and waiting, they are ready from the word "go."

When you see the word Spaniel, think of a sentimentalist. Gentle and easy-going, Spaniel breeds love everyone and they enjoy being fussed over. Spaniels and the other members of the Sporting Group— the Pointers, Setters and Retrievers—make wonderful hunting companions. Because of their instinct to point, flush or retrieve birds, Sporting breeds are apt to roam.

Hound breeds are of two kinds. Sight Hounds—such as the Greyhound, the Afghan Hound or the Saluki—track fur-bearing game by using their eyes. They are naturally quick-moving. Scent Hounds track man as well as other animals. They are slower moving and they instinctively have their nose to the ground. To train a Scent Hound

—such as the Bloodhound, the Bassett or the Beagle—to walk with his head in the air, can sometimes be a problem.

For guard work or herding, certain breeds perform better than others. Among the Working breeds, the German Shepherd Dog, the Doberman Pinscher, the Briard or the Giant Schnauzer are good examples of guard dogs. However, any large dog would be worth considering if you want a dog for protection. Size alone should frighten unwelcome intruders. So can the excessive barking of a small dog. For herding, the instinct is strong in Collies, Shetland Sheepdogs, Border Collies and Welsh Corgis.

Size is an important factor when buying a dog. Large dogs eat more than small dogs. There is the question of exercise and whether one has the ability to handle a dog of weight. But most large dogs are gentle and they make clean house pets.

Breeds with a short, flat, "pushed-in" nose will sniffle and snore more than breeds with a long head. Those with loose jowls will drool more than those with tight lips. Breeds with straight coats, whether long or short, unless the coat is of the wool variety, such as that of the Poodle or the Kerry Blue Terrier, will shed. Long hair requires grooming, and in the case of the Poodle and most Terrier breeds, unless you do the clipping or trimming yourself, there is the cost of professional coat care.

Will the dog live outdoors where he needs coat protection, or will he be a house-pet where coat is less important? Will he live in a hot climate where the Bulldog, for instance, might be uncomfortable? A Chihuahua, on the other hand, enjoys heat and sunshine.

The following guide will help you select your breed of dog. It rates each breed as a pet, with emphasis on size, care, temperament and training. Select your dog wisely.

VERY SMALL BREEDS	Weight: 4 to 12 pounds; height: 5 to 11 inches at top of shoulder back of neck. Recommended for apartment living, for people who travel and for those who want a lap dog. Exercise is no problem.
Affenpinscher	Bright, alert, friendly. Little grooming. Coat dense and wiry. Pert, Terrier spirit. Rare breed. Fearless toward aggressor.
Bichon Frise	Beautiful disposition. Profuse, silky and loosely-curled coat. Requires extensive grooming to maintain desired "powder-puff" appearance.
Brussels Griffon	Easy to train. Little grooming. One coat variety smooth; one wiry. Reserved, sensitive nature. Hardy, spirited.
Chihuahua (Smooth)	Affectionate. Intelligent. Seldom roams. Short, glossy coat requires little grooming. Smallest of all dogs. Enjoys sunshine and heat. Slow to accept other breeds of dogs.
Chihuahua (Long-coated)	Affectionate. Not quarrelsome. Easy to train. Less clannish than the smooth variety. Coat long, silky, requires some grooming.
English Toy Spaniel	Extremely affectionate and good-tempered. Long, silky coat requires grooming.
Italian Greyhound	Gentle to care for. Calm, affectionate. Short, glossy coat requires little grooming. Seldom bathed. Not a yapper. One hardly knows there is a dog around unless his deep voice gives warning.
Japanese Spaniel	Well-mannered. Affectionate. Agile. Has definite likes and dislikes. Long, silky hair requires grooming.
Maltese	Lively, friendly, hardy. Adaptable to town or country. Long, silky hair requires extensive grooming.
Manchester Terrier (Toy)	Alert, clean house pet. Doesn't shed. Short, smooth coat.
Miniature Dachshund (Smooth) (Wirehaired) (Longhaired)	Responsive. Affectionate. Little grooming. Playful. Amusing. Longhaired variety requires some grooming.
Miniature Pinscher	Trains easily. Short, glossy coat requires little grooming. Good watch dog. Favors home and master.
Papillon	Anxious to please. Withstands both heat and cold. Excellent for country or city. Medium-short coat requires some grooming.
Pekingese	Bold, loyal, self-reliant. Faithful companion. Breed with definite likes and dislikes. Long, thick, silky coat requires extra grooming.

Pomeranian	A happy, alert, sturdy dog with stamina. Not quarrelsome. A guard dog that means business. Profuse, long, shiny coat requires extra grooming.
Toy Manchester Terrier	Alert. Clean house pet. Doesn't shed. Short, glossy coat requires little grooming.
Toy Poodle	Trains easily. Anxious to please. Companionable. No doggie odor. Doesn't shed. Upkeep expensive. Requires extensive grooming as well as professional clipping every 4 to 6 weeks.
Silky Terrier	Friendly. Spirited. Has sense of humor. Medium-long, silky hair requires grooming.
Yorkshire Terrier	Not a delicate lap dog. Highly intelligent. Possesses Terrier spirit and independence. Long, silky hair requires grooming.
SMALL BREEDS	Weight: 11 to 32 pounds; height: 9 to 20 inches. Suitable for small apartments. Exercise a minor factor.
Australian Terrier	Companionable. Easy to train. Harsh, wiry coat requires little grooming. Not a noisy dog.
Basenji	Clean house pet. While he doesn't bark, he does chortle. Short coat requires little grooming. Likes children. Playful, yet suspicious of the unusual.
Beagle	Good rabbit dog. Gentle, not quarrelsome. Short, flat coat requires little grooming. Sensitive nature. Like most Hound breeds, he always has his nose to the ground.
Bedlington Terrier	Quiet house pet. Doesn't shed. Affectionate. Fine, woolly coat requires special trimming.
Border Terrier	Friendly. Hardy, great courage and stamina. Harsh, dense, wiry coat requires little grooming. A fairly rare breed.
Boston Terrier	Sweet with people. Clean house pet. Short coat requires little grooming. Great home protector. Not yappy.
Cairn Terrier	Alert, adapts to town or country. Quieter than most Terriers. Profuse coat requires grooming but no professional trimming.

Cocker Spaniel	An alert family dog. As a rule, friendly toward both people and dogs. The silky, flat coat requires special trimming for show.
Dachshund **(Smooth)** **(Wirehaired)** **(Longhaired)**	Responsive. Lively. Playful. Amusing. Little grooming, except Longhaired variety, which requires some grooming. Somewhat a one-man dog.
Dandie Dinmont **Terrier**	Clean, obedient house pet. Intelligent. Patient with children. Medium-short coat requires some grooming but no professional trimming.
English Cocker **Spaniel**	A sensible fellow. Friendly. Affectionate. Flat, silky coat requires professional touch-up.
Fox Terrier **(Smooth)**	Friendly. Quick to learn. Smooth coat requires little grooming. A courageous, energetic sport. Good trick dog.
(Wire)	Good-natured toward people. Keen, sporty disposition. Requires professional trimming.
French Bulldog	Sweet-tempered, clean house pet. Short, smooth coat requires little grooming.
Irish Terrier	Country or city dog. Good with children. High spirited. Unflinching courage. Dense, wiry coat requires professional trimming.
Lakeland Terrier	Less excitable than most Terriers. Hard, dense, wiry coat requires professional trimming.
Lhasa Apso	Responsive. Trains easily. Good watch dog. Heavy, long coat requires extra grooming.
Manchester Terrier	Alert. Clean house pet. Doesn't shed. Short, smooth coat requires little grooming. One-man watch dog.
Miniature Poodle	Trains easily. Anxious to please. Companionable. No doggie odor. Doesn't shed. Upkeep expensive. Requires extensive grooming as well as professional clipping every 4 to 6 weeks.
Miniature Schnauzer	Companionable. Alert. Playful. Harsh, wiry coat requires professional trimming.
Norwich Terrier	Lovable. Not a quarrelsome breed. Dense, medium-short coat requires grooming but needs no trimming.
Pug	Friendly. Companionable. Clean house pet. Smooth, short coat needs little grooming.
Schipperke	Alert. Trains easily. Coat, while abundant, requires little grooming. Faithful watch dog.

Scottish Terrier	Devoted to master. Sturdy with independent disposition. Dense, wiry coat requires special trimming.
Sealyham Terrier	Friendly toward people and dogs. Intelligent. Has a sense of humor. Dense, harsh, wiry coat requires special trimming.
Shetland Sheepdog	Obedient and affectionate. Good with children. Loves family life. Delights in guarding property and giving warning. Medium-long, dense coat requires grooming.
Shih Tzu	Hardy. Town or country. Affectionate. Loyal. Alert. Small breed. Playful. Long, woolly coat requires grooming.
Skye Terrier	Possesses acute vision and hearing. Game-to-the-death Terrier. Long coat (5 to 6 inches) requires extensive grooming.
Tibetan Terrier	Not actually a Terrier—traditionally a companion dog. Exceptionally healthy with delightful temperament. Profuse coat, either straight or waved.
Welsh Corgi (Cardigan)	Good with children. Adapts to town or country. Dense coat requires little grooming.
(Pembroke)	Pleasing temperament. Responsive. Herding instinct.
Welsh Terrier	Not a quarrelsome breed. Likes town or country. Reliable with children. Wiry, close-fitting coat requires special trimming.
West Highland White Terrier	Friendly toward people and dogs. Hardy. Self-assured. Independent. Hard, stiff coat requires grooming but no professional trimming.
Whippet	Obedient. Untroublesome. Smooth, short coat. Little grooming. Never snappy or barky. One hardly knows there is a dog around.

14

MEDIUM-SIZED BREEDS	Weight: 35 to 60 pounds; height: 12 to 23 inches. Recommended for both country and city. Exercise is a factor.
Airedale Terrier	Friendly. Amiable playmate for children. Good family dog. Short, harsh, dense coat requires professional trimming. Fine guard dog.
American Staffordshire Terrier	Short coat. Little grooming. Powerful. Requires firm handling. Originally bred for fighting, now docile.
American Water Spaniel	Good hunting companion. Fine family dog. Affectionate. Tightly curled coat requires some grooming.
Basset Hound	Friendly. Gentle. Short, dense coat. Little grooming.
Bearded Collie	An ancient British sheepdog, still very much valued on farms. Good temperament. Double coat—outer coat harsh, strong and flat. Requires grooming.
Brittany Spaniel	Even-tempered. Companionable. Dense, flat coat requires little grooming. A hunting dog that both points and retrieves birds. Sensitive nature.
Bulldog	Reliable with children. Sweet with people. Patient. Flat, smooth coat.
Bull Terrier (White) (Colored)	Friendly toward people. Patient. Short, flat coat. Little grooming. Sensitive spirit. Powerful but amenable.
Chow Chow	Devoted to master. A one-man dog. Dense, woolly coat requires extra grooming.
Clumber Spaniel	Sedate. Lovable. Silky, dense coat, even with fringes, requires little grooming. Good hunting companion when speed is not essential. Rare breed.
Dalmatian	A versatile breed. Used for many purposes. Short, sleek coat. Little grooming. Not noisy. Carefree. Happy-go-lucky, yet capable of guard work.
English Springer Spaniel	A cheerful fellow. Friendly. Loving. Flat, medium-length coat requires little grooming. Professional trimming for show.
Field Spaniel	Friendly. Loving. Flat, silky hair requires little grooming. A hunting dog of moderate speed but great perseverance. Rare breed.
Harrier	Short, dense coat requires little grooming. A reliable hunting dog. Not a numerous breed.
Keeshond	Responsive. Anxious to please. Friendly. Likes children. Withstands cold. Sheds. Dense, thick coat requires grooming. Sensitive spirit.
Kerry Blue Terrier	Trustworthy with children. Doesn't shed. Soft, dense coat requires professional trimming.

15

Norwegian Elkhound	Sweet-tempered without nerves. Hardy. Courageous. Energetic. Thick, woolly coat requires grooming.
Puli	Gentle with children. Devoted, home-loving companion. A good watch dog. Long, fine hair requires extensive grooming.
Samoyed	Polite. Well-behaved. As in the case of all arctic breeds, no doggie odor. Good with children. Strong, alert, graceful. Thick, profuse coat requires grooming.
Siberian Husky	Friendly. Good for city or country. Free of doggie odor. Alert, graceful. Sled dog.
Soft-Coated Wheaten Terrier	Originally a hunter of small game and guard dog. Steady, spirited and with strong stamina. Coat soft and wavy, and for showing is not to be clipped, plucked, or stylized.
Staffordshire Bull Terrier	Lighter in weight than the American Staffordshire. Smooth coat and with great strength for its size. Little grooming.
Standard Schnauzer	Sensible. Even-tempered. Good with children. Guard dog. Hard, wiry coat requires professional trimming for show.
Staffordshire Terrier	Reliable with children. Short coat. Little grooming. Powerful. Requires firm handling. Originally bred for fighting, now docile.
Sussex Spaniel	Pleasant. Companionable. Cheerful and tractable. A hunting dog. Flat coat with fringes requires some grooming.
Welsh Springer Spaniel	Amiable. Flat, silky coat. Little grooming. Retrieves both on land and water. Rare breed.
Wirehaired Pointing Griffon	Versatile. Easy-going. Hard, stiff coat. Little grooming. Not a numerous breed.

LARGE BREEDS	Weight: 55 to 75 pounds; height: 23 to 27 inches. Recommended for country living. For city living under certain conditions. Exercise a factor.
Akita	A Japanese hunting breed. Short, dense coat. Requires little grooming.
Afghan Hound	Withstands both heat and cold. Gentle by nature. Not snappish. Reserved. Prefers his own family. Not a noisy breed. Long, fine, silky hair requires extra grooming.
Alaskan Malamute	Gentle. Friendly. Woolly, thick, coarse coat requires little grooming. A sled dog, noted for pulling power and endurance.
American Foxhound	Friendly toward people. Short coat. Little grooming. A sporting dog with stamina.

Belgian Malinois	A large dog. Alert. Trainable for guard work. Devoted to master.
Belgian Sheepdog Belgian Tervuren	Alert. Devoted to master. Trainable for police work. Distrustful of strangers. Short to long, straight coat requires some grooming.
Bernese Mountain Dog	A good-natured "draft-horse." Withstands cold. Long, silky coat requires grooming. Little known breed.
Black and Tan Coonhound	Friendly. Gentle. Not quarrelsome. Short coat requires little grooming. A sporting dog that enjoys his work.
Boxer	Excellent with children. Clean house pet. Short coat. Little grooming. Playful. Suspicious of the unusual. Possesses rugged strength with ability to defend.
Briard	Has sharp sense of hearing and an unusually good memory. A family dog. Of a serious nature. Long coat requires grooming. Little bathing.
Chesapeake Bay Retriever	A retrieving dog that withstands rough, icy water. One of the best of all dogs with children. Powerfully built. Alert and willing to work.
Collie (Rough)	Friendly. Responsive. Trains easily. Not quarrelsome. Coat abundant. Requires care.
(Smooth)	Friendly. Responsive. Trains easily. Little coat care. Quite rare.
Curly-Coated Retriever	Willing. Trains easily. Sweet-tempered. Retrieves both from land and water. Dense mass of crisp, short curls requires grooming.
Doberman Pinscher	Trains easily. Smooth, short coat. Little grooming. Unafraid but mind their own business. Guard and police dog. Devoted to home and family.
English Foxhound	Affectionate. Responsive. Short, dense coat. Little grooming. Hunts as a part of a pack. As a pet, gentle.
English Setter	Gentle. Patient with children. Sensitive. Flat, silky coat requires professional "touch-up" for show.
Flat-Coated Retriever	Sensible. Obedient. Dense, flat coat. Little grooming. Retrieves both on land and water. Rare breed.
German Shepherd Dog	Intelligent. Devoted to family. Generally thought of as a "one-man" or "one-family" dog. Dense, close-lying coat requires some grooming.
German Shorthaired Pointer	Versatile sporting dog. Short coat. Little grooming. Mild manner. Not quarrelsome.

German Wirehaired Pointer	Companionable family dog. Harsh, wiry coat. Little grooming.
Giant Schnauzer	Intelligent. Willing. Close, strong, wiry coat. Little grooming. Used for guard and police work. Very reliable.
Golden Retriever	Gentle. Affectionate. Even-tempered. Trains easily. Good with children. Sheds a fair amount. Dense, water-resisting coat requires some grooming.
Gordon Setter	Gentle. Affectionate. Trains easily. One-man dog. Versatile as a sporting dog. Soft, silky coat with fringes, requires some grooming.
Greyhound	Gentle. Devoted. Short, smooth coat. Little grooming. Quiet in the home. One hardly knows there is a dog around.
Irish Setter	Gentle. Affectionate. Seldom resentful or aggressive. Happy-go-lucky. Carefree. Medium-short, flat, silky coat with fringes. Some grooming. Touch-up for show.
Irish Water Spaniel	Likable, all-round dog. Mass of tight, crisp, ringlets, requires grooming.
Kuvasz	Strongly home-loving. Seldom strays. Watch dog. Herd dog. Dense coat of medium length requires some grooming.
Labrador Retriever	Hardy. Devoted to people. Anxious to please. Short, dense coat. Little grooming. Powerfully built.
Old English Sheepdog	Excellent with children. Seldom fights. Seldom roams. Good for town or country. Has a sense of humor. Long, heavy coat requires extensive grooming.
Otter Hound	Sweet-natured. Wise. Hard, crisp, oily coat. Little grooming. Not a numerous breed.
Pointer	Works well for more than one master. Short, flat coat. Little grooming. Independent, alert. Has great stamina in the field.
Saluki	Affectionate. Withstands any climate. Little grooming. A quiet, lovable pet.
Standard Poodle	Trains easily. Anxious to please. Companionable. No doggie odor. Doesn't shed. Upkeep expensive. Requires extensive grooming as well as professional clipping every 4 to 6 weeks. Excellent with children.
Vizsla	A large dog with an excellent nose. Coat short, smooth. Bird dog of moderate speed.
Weimaraner	Intelligent. Energetic. Short, smooth coat. Little grooming. A hunting dog with great power and stamina.

VERY LARGE BREEDS	Weight: 90 to 185 pounds; height: 25 to 33 inches. Recommended for country living. Exercise a major factor.
Bloodhound	Gentle. Affectionate. Short, smooth coat. Little grooming. "Sniffy"—that's his job!
Borzoi	Gentle. Graceful. Quiet. Light on leash. Long, silky coat requires grooming.
Bouvier des Flandres	Level-headed. Capable. Tousled short coat requires little grooming. Rare breed in United States.
Bullmastiff	Sensible. Short, dense coat. Little grooming. Guard dog. Gives protection without savagery.
Great Dane	Friendly toward people. Short, smooth coat. Little grooming. Spirited, courageous, dependable.
Great Pyrenees	A home-loving dog. Sweet with people. Especially children. Intelligent. Guard dog. Thick, heavy coat requires grooming.
Irish Wolfhound	A peaceful house pet. Courteous and gentle. Even-tempered. Devoted. Tallest of all breeds. A quiet dog. Wiry, harsh coat. Some grooming.
Komondor	Self-reliant. Guard dog. Distrustful of strangers. Woolly coat requires extra grooming. Not a numerous breed.
Mastiff	Devoted family dog. Good-natured, courageous, docile. Short coat. Little grooming. Heaviest of all breeds.
Newfoundland	Lovable, gentle. Responsive. Intelligent. The canine "lifeguard." Heavy, dense, oily, water-proof coat requires grooming.
Rhodesian Ridgeback	Devoted family dog. Never noisy or quarrelsome. Short, flat coat. Little grooming. The hair grows the wrong way in a ridge down the back. Not so well-known as some other breeds.
Rottweiler	Affectionate. Obedient. Steady disposition. Short coat. Little grooming. Guard dog. Herder.
St. Bernard	Gentle with people. Has an uncanny sense of smell and of approaching danger. Dense, moderately long, flat coat requires grooming.
Scottish Deerhound	Devoted, polite, pleasant house pet. Desires human companionship. Harsh, wiry coat (3 to 4 inches) requires grooming.

BREEDS LISTED IN THE "MISCELLANEOUS" CLASS BY THE AMERICAN KENNEL CLUB

Note: There are currently 122 breeds accepted for registration in the Stud Book by the American Kennel Club. The AKC does not, per se, encourage the admittance of new breeds. However, it does provide for a regular method of development which may result in such recognition. When in the judgment of the AKC's Board of Directors there is a substantial nationwide interest and activity in a breed—including an active parent club maintaining a breed registry, with serious and expanding breed activity over a wide geographical area—a breed may be admitted to the Miscellaneous Class.

Miscellaneous breeds may be shown in Obedience competition, and can win Obedience titles. However, in conformation shows, they can only compete in the Miscellaneous class, and cannot win championship points. When the Board of Directors is satisfied that a breed is showing a healthy, dynamic growth in the Miscellaneous class, it may be admitted to registration in the Stud Book, and the opportunity to compete for championships.

Australian Cattle Dog	A medium-sized herding dog. Previously known as the Australian Heeler because it keeps herds in check by nipping at heels of strays. Short, slightly harsh coat requires little grooming.
Australian Kelpie	Abundant, long, hard coat. Some grooming. Small herding dog.
Border Collie	Obedient. Alert. Agile. Herding dog of medium size, with stamina.
Cavalier King Charles Spaniel	Extremely affectionate. Good tempered. Long, silky coat requires grooming.
Ibizan Hound	Ancient Egyptian hunting and racing breed. Large in height, but medium in weight. Short coat requires little grooming.
Miniature Bull Terrier	Strongly built small breed. Amenable to discipline. Short, harsh coat requires little grooming.
Spinoni Italiana	Withstands all weather. Coat rough. Short. Little grooming. Dog of medium size.

THE PUPPY'S EARLY TRAINING

A well brought up dog is obviously more pleasant to have around than one that can only be termed a general nuisance. Yet, the majority of dog owners neglect their dog's early education, so vital to good upbringing. Dogs by the hundreds of thousands chase automobiles, keep neighborhoods awake with senseless barking, leap with dirty paws on immaculate guests, bite delivery boys and postmen, ruin furniture, and make walking them on a leash a tense, tangled, arm-straining ordeal.

Teaching a dog to behave is really not hard or complicated. All it normally requires is patience, an understanding of the dog, and simple training techniques that follow a basic pattern.

HOW DOES A DOG LEARN?

A dog learns, not through her * rudimentary reasoning power, but by associating pleasant or unpleasant consequences with her behavior. She obeys commands or signals when they are connected with such associations in her mind. And after the trainer repeats the commands or signals often enough for the dog's reactions to become habitual, the dog may properly be termed obedient.

A dog is best educated through praise and gentle scolding, and through the proper use of the collar and leash for routine obedience training. Tell the average dog what you want, and when you help her to obey, she will cooperate willingly. It is only the problem dogs that require special handling. But in any case, correcting or disciplining must be done at the time or immediately after the dog errs so she will understand the reason for the punishment. She must be corrected every time the mistake is made so she will associate the punishment with her act.

* Note: Throughout this book the dog is referred to as **her**, in the interest of simplicity. This does not mean that male dogs are poor performers or any more difficult to train than females.

WHEN SHOULD TRAINING BE STARTED?

The dog training may be started as early as four or five months of age, but before we get into formal education, here are some things every puppy should learn:

To Stay Alone Quietly

Whether you acquired your puppy at six weeks or at four months of age, teach her to stay by herself. Shut her in a room, then close the door. If she barks or scratches to get out, toss something at the door that will make a loud noise. If the barking or scratching continues, toss it again. Do this at intervals until the puppy will learn to stay by herself without making a fuss. After the puppy gets used to daytime solitude, she will adjust more quickly to staying alone at night. A dog that hasn't been trained to stay alone will usually bark, chew, or deliberately wet when you leave her.

Not To Jump On People

While committed in the friendliest of spirits, one of dogs' most irritating social errors is jumping on people. Every time your puppy comes running, spread your fingers fan-like and say "NO

JUMPING!" If she jumps up in spite of the warning, bump her nose once to make her get down. Then pat her. You can also lift your knee when your dog jumps up, but the spread fingers with the warning "No jumping!" is more effective.

To Keep Off Furniture

Start by pushing the puppy down every time she tries to get on the furniture. Use a stern "NO!" If she sneaks up when you are out of the room, place something in her favorite chair that will squawk or make some other loud noise. A wound-up toy or a crackly paper should do the trick.

Not To Steal Food

Leave food where the puppy can reach it. When she tries to sniff it, call out sharply "NO!" If necessary, tap her gently on the nose to remind her. If the habit still persists, toss something so it lands close to the food she is reaching for. One or two experiences should cure the habit of stealing.

Not To Chase Cars

If you are driving the car, stop and chase the puppy home. If this is ineffective, carry two or three small empty cartons in the car and while chasing her, toss the cartons in back of her. If the puppy is broken to collar and leash, work with a friend. Ask the friend to blast the car horn when he approaches, then forcefully jerk the puppy away from in front of the car so she will learn to respect moving vehicles.

Not To Chew, Bark, Or Wet

Chewing, barking, and wetting in the house are cured more quickly when you catch the puppy doing wrong. The first few times, call out sharply "NO!" and stop her from doing mischief. If she persists in spite of the warning, drop some small object close by and surprise her in the act. A wire cage, available at most kennel supply shops, where you can keep the puppy when you can't watch her, will simplify raising a young puppy. Learning to stay quietly alone in her own little house is an important part of a puppy's training. She will also be where she can't do damage.

SIMPLE OBEDIENCE TRAINING (FOUR TO FIVE MONTHS)

Begin simple training by introducing the puppy to her collar—a leather one—and her leash. Play with her. Let her drag the leash on the ground. Avoid the unpleasantness resulting from jerking the leash too hard or forcefully dragging the puppy around.

Lesson 1. Walking Without Pulling On The Leash

Don't expect your young puppy to ALWAYS walk at heel position as required in Obedience Trials, but teach her to walk **without pulling.** Every time she darts ahead, say "Heel!" (she might as well learn this word from the beginning), tug backward on the leash, then pat your side to encourage her to walk there. If she darts ahead a second time, stand still and repeat the action. When she walks with leash slack, praise her, and tell her, "Good girl!"

If the puppy won't walk at all, kneel and tap your fingers on the ground. Coax her with praise. If she still refuses to walk, **slowly** and **gently** drag her while you give continuous praise. When the puppy no longer grovels but gets to her feet, slacken the leash and clap your hands for encouragement.

Lesson 2. The Sit

When you want your puppy to sit, hold her head up with the leash in one hand, say "Sit!" and while you push on her hindquarters with the other hand to make her sit, tell her "Good Girl!" After she is sitting, pat her.

Later, instead of pushing on the hindquarters, tap them lightly to make her sit more quickly. Remember to say "Sit!" before you spank her to a sitting position, so she will learn the meaning of the word.

Lesson 3. Staying When Told

A young puppy won't stay for long when the owner is some distance away. She can, however, be taught to stay on the grooming table or to stay on command the length of the leash. Put the puppy on a low bench or table and tell her "Stay!" If she tries to jump off, put her back and tell her "Stay!" again. When she gets off the table, it should be with your permission.

For leash training, with the puppy sitting at your left side, place your left hand in front of her muzzle and tell her "Stay!" After you say it, step forward on your right foot. If she follows, grab the leash and quickly put her back where she was. If she stays when you tell her, turn and face her, then slowly circle to your right, around and in back of her. At first you may have to use both hands to keep her sitting.

Lesson 4. Coming When Called

The object here is to teach the puppy the meaning of the word "Come!" This is accomplished through timing the command with the use of the leash, then giving a generous reward for coming. With the puppy on leash, call her name and tell her "Come!" whether she is looking at you or not. After you call, tug once on the leash, then clap your hands to encourage her to come quickly. If you are working with a small dog, kneel when you call her. Do this until your puppy will turn and run toward you when she hears you call.

Lesson 5. **To Lie Down**

Avoid roughness when you make your puppy lie down. Move slowly and handle gently. There are different ways you can make a puppy lie down. You can pull down on the collar and press lightly on her shoulders or hindquarters. You can trip the puppy by turning both her back legs to one side to make her lie on one hip. You can reach over the puppy's back and slide the front legs forward. The important things to remember: give the command first, and while you are putting the puppy down slowly, praise her or scratch her gently with your fingers.

Lesson 6. **To Stand**

With the puppy on leash, pull the leash **forward** with one hand while you tickle her under the stomach with the other. At the same time, say "Stand!" After she is standing, scratch her back and if she tries to sit down, reach under her stomach and lift her gently. A dog that learns to stand on command is easier to groom.

THE NOVICE OBEDIENCE COURSE

Four Important Reasons Why Your Dog Should Be Trained:

1. For your own pleasure, comfort, and satisfaction
2. For your dog's happiness, well-being, and safety
3. To avoid annoyance to your friends and neighbors
4. For the good of your community

A trained dog may be qualified to enter Obedience Trials at dog shows and win Obedience Degrees.

A TRAINED DOG IS A HAPPY DOG!

THE DOG IN TRAINING

The dog in training should be in good physical condition and given the necessary inoculations to safeguard health.

Before each training session:

Feed lightly

Exercise

Give a small amount of water

Groom, for both comfort and appearances' sake

Having attended to your dog's needs, be serious, but not domineering, about the training.

Dog training is divided into two phases: (1) teaching, and (2) employing corrective techniques to overcome problems. There is no **one** way to train a dog, nor do two dogs react to training in exactly the same way, but owners who are interested in training their dogs for Obedience competition should keep the following in mind: during basic training, first consideration should be for the dog and not the rule book. After the dog has learned to work happily and with spirit, the handler should condition himself for the Obedience ring by eliminating double commands, body motions and extra praise used while teaching. When making corrections, he should also keep in mind that the manner in which corrections are made is what counts.

TRAINING SUGGESTIONS

When you teach voice commands, give the command then follow with the **signal,** and the **correction** and the **praise** simultaneously.

When you teach hand signals, give the signal then follow with the **voice,** and the **correction** and the **praise** together.

When you want your dog to come, call her name, give the command and follow the command with **praise.** While she is coming, clap your hands to cheer her on.

When your dog is some distance away and you want her to obey a command (for instance, to stay), stress the command without using her name. The name may bring her to you.

Give a command ONCE! If you repeat the command, put a correction with it.

Praise must be discontinued when exhibiting in Obedience Trials but if used AFTER every command and WITH every correction during the training period, your dog will be more responsive.

When you praise, BE SINCERE! Dogs respond to a cajoling tone of voice.

Modify your method of training to the SIZE AND TEMPERAMENT of the dog. All dogs do not train alike!

When you correct for a problem, disguise corrections so you, the trainer, will not appear responsible.

Don't overdo corrections. Start gently until you see how YOU dog reacts.

If your training efforts are NOT successful, be more demanding When you correct for a REPEATED mistake, use a firmer tone o voice and jerk the leash harder.

Strive for perfection from the beginning. When you are careles about little things, they become problems later on.

If you are a woman and prefer to train in a dress, select one with out too much flare. Training a small dog necessitates stooping or bend ing. A full skirt will get in the dog's way.

In Obedience Trials, you cannot use your dog's name when you giv a hand signal. In other words, you cannot say "Robin!" and motio your dog to come or to go-to-heel. In your early training, avoid usin your dog's name when you give a signal.

You cannot give a hand signal with a voice command EXCEP when you leave your dog alone. In this case, you can say "Stay!" an make a motion with your hand, but you CANNOT say "Robin, stay!' and give the signal.

At the start of heeling and after every halt, use your dog's nam with the heeling command to get her attention.

Condition your dog for the Open Course by encouraging her, durin basic training, to carry assorted articles, to retrieve thrown objects and to leap small hurdles. This early training paves the way for th advanced work, without affecting the dog's skill while competing i the Novice Classes.

The instructions given in the succeeding sections of this book ar for people who are right-handed. Those who are left-handed may fol low the same instructions, simply substituting the left hand for th right and the right hand for the left.

USE THE PROPER TRAINING EQUIPMENT! This may be a leather, nylon, or chain slip collar and a six-foot flat leather leash with a strong snap. The type of collar and size of leash vary with the breed and with the temperament of the dog. If your dog is gentle, use a plain, round leather collar.

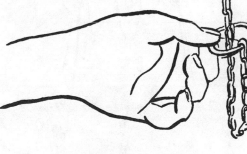

How to make collar

PRACTICE HOW TO HOLD THE LEASH! Loop the handle around the palm of your right hand and take hold of the leash with the left hand, above the dog's head. Bring your right hand to your waist and grasp the leash in the center. Hold both arms close to the body and keep the left elbow straight. (See illustration.)

When you hold the leash this way, you can make heeling corrections with a minimum of hand motion.

LEARN HOW TO PUT ON THE SLIP COLLAR! With the dog on your left side, the leash fastens to the ring of the chain that passes OVER the dog's neck. If on correctly, the collar will click when you snap the leash and will loosen when you slacken it. (See illustrations.)

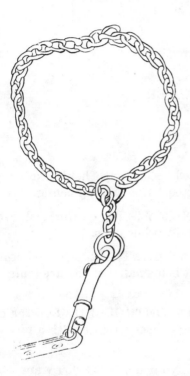

*The right collar
loosens automatically.*

*The wrong collar stays tight
all the time.*

Note: in Obedience Trials a dog is required to walk at the handler's left.

THE TRAINER

KEEP YOUR DOG'S ATTENTION. Play with her! Nudge her when she looks away. Make unexpected turns while heeling.

DON'T LET YOUR DOG BE "SNIFFY." Tug on the leash every time she lowers her head or tries to sniff other dogs.

DON'T LET YOUR DOG LUNGE AT ANOTHER DOG. Threaten her with a small, rolled magazine. If it is a small dog you are training, drop the magazine at her feet.

DON'T LET YOUR DOG BARK UNCONTROLLED. Pull the collar tight and cuff her nose. In persistent cases, muzzle with a piece of 2-inch gauze bandage.

TIME YOUR CORRECTIONS. Tell your dog what you want, then use the leash to help her do it.

CORRECT WITH A MINIMUM OF HAND MOTION. Don't **drag** on the leash. Snap it!

USE THE PROPER TONE OF VOICE—a normal tone for first commands, a demanding tone (without yelling) when the dog disobeys.

KEEP YOUR DOG HAPPY. Give praise after every command and every time you use the leash. If you train in a rough manner, it will show in your dog's attitude.

*A tap on the hindquarters with the right
foot will keep your dog attentive.*

HEELING

With the leash in both hands (with the left elbow straight and both arms close to your body), command "Robin, heel!" **After you give the command,** move forward on your left foot, snap the leash forward, pat your side and give praise. Timing and praise are important! If your dog darts ahead, STAND STILL. Snap the leash backward, again giving praise. Make left U-turns every few feet (both handler and dog turn to the left), and if your dog still forges, lift your knee and bump her chest. If it is a small dog you are training, use the inside of your right foot to push her around on the turns. Praise when you make these corrections.

Alternate the left U-turn with the right-about turn. Pivot sharply **without slackening speed and without dragging on the leash.** After you turn, snap the leash forward, then again pat your side.

Include a fast and a slow pace in the heeling exercise. When you run, jerk the leash forward **with praise.** When you slow to a walk, jerk the leash backward, giving praise. Use short, quick snaps.

Circle continuously to the right, then circle continuously to the left. Follow the circling with a zigzag pattern. A change of direction will keep your dog attentive.

By now the heeling routine should include right-angle and left-angle turns. Pivot sharply without slackening speed and tug on the leash **after** you turn. Practice the Figure 8. Circle two posts, two chairs, or two of anything, placed 6 to 8 feet apart. Teach your dog to change pace as you did in the heeling exercise (see above). Do this by speeding up when the dog is on the outside of the circle, and jerking the leash forward in a series of snaps while giving praise. Slow to a walk when the dog is on the inside of the circle, then speed up again when she is on the outside, this time without jerking the leash. Give praise as before.

Continue the heeling routine with the handle of the leash over your shoulder and with your arms at your side. WALK BRISKLY! Never adapt your pace to that of the dog. At the first sign of carelessness, use a demanding "HEEL!" and jerk the leash harder. Follow corrections with a few words of praise.

When heeling with the leash over the shoulder is nearly perfect, permit your dog to heel free. Carry the leash, wadded up, in your right hand. Hold your left hand close to your side and encourage the dog by gently patting your thigh. If your dog stays close and heels nicely, let her know you are pleased by praising her while she is working. If she breaks away, STAND STILL. Use a demanding tone when you repeat the heeling command and if she still ignores it and starts running around, throw the leash at her heels to make her listen. Kneel, and tell her "COME!" After she comes, snap the leash on her collar, and make sharper corrections.

If you are working with a large dog that is slow to come around on the about-turn, put the dog on leash. Wad the handle of the leash into a ball and carry it in your left hand. When you make the about-turn, reach back with your right hand and spank the dog playfully on the rump. After you spank her, clap your hands so the dog will think the correction was in fun. If you do it carefully, you can use your right foot instead of your hand, but don't make the correction too often.

When teaching your dog to heel, make the training a game. Use playful corrections when possible and give adequate praise so your dog will enjoy the heeling exercise.

HEELING Problems—How To Overcome Them

Lags While Heeling

Put the dog on leash and make corrections whether you think the dog needs them or not. In other words, don't go through the heeling routine just holding the leash. After every change of direction and change of pace, snap the leash forward, giving praise. Do this two or three times, then give praise when you turn, without jerking the leash.

If temperament permits, an assistant can sometimes walk behind the dog and gently tap her with a light rod every time she drops back. Tapping the floor with the rod will sometimes speed up a lagging dog. After these corrections, the owner must encourage the dog to stay close through praise and patting.

Wide On The Right-About Turn

With your dog on leash and sitting at heel position, do a series of about-turns from a standstill. When you turn, reach back with your **right** foot and tap the dog gently on her right flank. Halt, and immediately pat her. If you are working with a small dog, assume a crouched position in order to have the hands on level with the dog. During the heeling routine, pivot sharply and do a complete circle to the right. When the leash is off, make playful corrections by spanking the large dog on the rear.

Dog Heels On Wrong Side

When the dog comes in on the wrong side, reach back with your **right** hand and cuff her once on the nose. Pat your left leg with your left hand to encourage her to come there. If you are working with a small dog, carry something firm but soft, that will just clear the floor. Instead of using your hand, use the object to bump her nose.

Fails To Change Pace

Put the dog on leash. When you run, jerk the leash forward, giving praise. Slow down to a walk, then dash forward again.

HEELING Problems—How To Overcome Them

After two or three corrections, go into the running pace without jerking the leash, but give praise just as before. Hold your hands close to your body to avoid excessive arm motion.

Barks While Heeling

If the dog barks while on leash, tug on the leash forcefully and tell her "STOP!" If she barks off leash, carry something that you can throw at her feet, or have an assistant throw it. Most dogs bark when they do an exercise fast. Repeat the correction until your dog will go into a running pace without yapping.

Lags On The Figure 8

Repeat the exercise suggested in the training instructions. Hold the leash in **both** hands if it is a large dog, and in the left hand if it is a small dog. When the dog is on the inside of the circle, walk naturally. When she is on the outside, speed up and jerk the leash forward in a series of snaps, giving praise. The third or fourth time around, speed up without jerking the leash but give praise just the same. This will teach your dog to change pace, an important feature of the Figure 8.

Forges While Heeling

An assistant walks at the dog's left and holds the leash in BOTH hands if it is a large dog, or in the right hand if it is a small dog. The owner gives the heeling command and follows the command with praise. Each time the dog forges, the owner repeats the word "heel." The assistant then jerks the leash backward with force.

An assistant can walk backward in front of the owner who is heeling his dog. When the dog forges, the assistant can bang on the floor (if it is a wooden floor) with some object held in his hand, or drop something, such as a small empty carton, in front to block the dog.

HEELING Problems—How To Overcome Them

Dog Bites Hand Or Leash While Heeling

If it is a large dog, hold your left hand still. When the dog misbehaves, cuff her nose with the right hand. Tell her "Stop it!" If it is a small dog and she bites at the leash, shake the leash hard or tap her on the nose and tell her "Stop!"

Dog Jumps Up And Down While Heeling

Every time the dog jumps up, use the leash to throw her off balance. When all four feet are on the ground, praise and pat her.

Dog Springs At Handler, Growling And Biting

Handle calmly. Take the leash in BOTH hands. Hold the dog away from your body and lift the front feet off the ground. After she quiets down, command "Sit," then quietly pat her.

Avoid jerking the leash. Drag the dog *slowly*, giving continuous praise. While she takes a few steps, slacken the leash but continue with the praise. In stubborn cases, lean over and tap the ground or the floor as you pull the dog toward you.

Patting the hip encourages the dog after leash corrections.

An assistant helps train a dog to stay at heel

THE SIT

When you come to a halt, shorten the leash in your **right** hand. Pull the leash **up** and **backward**. Push down on the dog's hindquarters with the left hand. Say "Sit, good girl (or boy)!" Pat her with the same hand you used to push her to the sitting position.

If your dog braces herself and you haven't the strength to force her to sit, flip the handle of the leash across her rump, and after she is sitting, pat her.

After she knows the meaning of "Sit," make her sit quickly. "Spank" her to a sitting position, then pat her with the same hand you used to spank her. The dog may think you are generous with your praise, but you will get excellent results.

During the heeling routine, wad the handle of the leash into a ball and hold it in your left hand, with the left elbow straight. When you halt, bring your feet together but don't move your left arm. Wait and see what the dog does. If she passes your knee without sitting, snap the leash backward. If she continues to stand, spank her to a sit. If she sits without being corrected, praise her. Give her credit for doing a good job. In Obedience Trials, the dog must sit when you halt, without being told. Each time you correct for not sitting, make the correction harder.

Don't step into your dog when you halt. This will make her move away. If she sits wide, coax her to come close. If she sits at an angle, straighten her out! The sit should be square and facing straight ahead.

Teaching the SIT

THE SIT-STAY
(The Long Sit)

Now that your dog knows how to sit, practice the sit-stay. With your dog at heel position, hold your left hand in front of the dog's muzzle, say "Stay!" and step forward on your right foot. Don't use your dog's name. If she follows, cuff her once, gently, on the nose (if she is a large dog), or use the leash to jerk her back to a sitting position. Repeat the command in a more demanding tone of voice.

When you leave your dog, give the stay signal with the left hand. Hold the palm toward the dog's muzzle with fingers pointing to the floor. When you face your dog, turn your hands so the palms are again toward the dog's muzzle with fingers pointing down. With the hands in this position you can quickly correct any forward movement with a cuff under the chin or use the leash to jerk the dog backward to make her sit down.

Holding the leash, circle your dog several times while she is sitting. Return to heel position by going to your right and around in back of the dog. Hold the leash to your left so it doesn't wrap itself around the dog. If your dog moves before you give permission, repeat the command more demandingly, and when you correct, correct rather sharply. At first, you may have to use both hands to keep her sitting. Do not yell and do not become angry.

With your dog sitting, tell her "Stay!" Face her, and then try to pull her from the sitting position. Don't jerk the leash, just pull it taut. Your dog should settle back and refuse to move. If she does move, correct her with a gentle cuff under the chin and tell her again, "Stay!"

While practicing the sit-stay, stand behind your dog as well as in front of her. It is permissible for a dog to turn her head but not her body. Try putting the leash on the ground but keep it fastened to the dog's collar. If she moves without permission, step on the leash, grab it up quickly and put her back where she was. At the same time, change your tone of voice to a demanding "STAY!"

Take the leash off. Increase the distance and the length of time you leave the dog. Tempt her by running past her. Clap your hands or call to another dog. If she moves, correct her. Leave her in the sit-stay position while you prepare her dinner or load the car for an outing. Try going where she can't see you. All of these things will help make your dog reliable on the sit-stay.

Hand signal STAY from the side

Hand signal STAY from the front

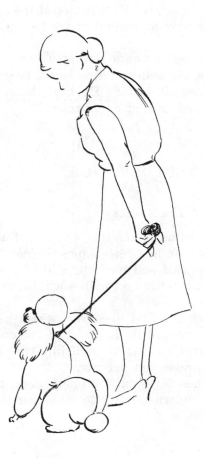

Feet should be together before you correct for slow sits or for sitting ahead.

SIT AND SIT-STAY Problems—How To Overcome Them

Slow To Sit On The Halt

While heeling, wad the handle of the leash into a ball and hold it in your left hand. Keep the elbow straight. Come to a halt and **after** your feet come together, jerk the leash backward with force, to make the dog sit quickly. Give praise at the same time. The important thing is to have no motion of the feet at the time you jerk the leash.

Alternate correction: an assistant walks at the dog's left. After the owner halts, the assistant spanks the large dog to a sitting position, to make her sit faster. He taps the small dog more gently. Both assistant and handler give praise.

Sits Ahead

Same as "Slow To Sit On The Halt."

Lies Down During The Sit-Stay

Fasten a long line to the dog's collar. Run the line through a ring placed four or five feet above the dog. Ask an assistant to stand off to one side and hold the end of the line. When the dog starts to lie down, a tug on the line will bring her to a sitting position.

To correct the dog that lies down when the leash is off, saunter back until you are directly in front of the dog, then quickly reach out with your foot and tap or scuff into the front paws. When the dog is sitting, praise and pat her.

If your dog lies down on a slippery floor, try sliding something along the floor underneath her to make her jump to a sitting position. Say "Sit!"

A tap on the rear with a small, rolled magazine
will speed up a large dog that is slow to sit.

SIT AND SIT-STAY Problems—How To Overcome Them

Sits At An Angle

An assistant walks at the dog's left. If the dog swings her hindquarters away from the handler, the assistant taps the dog gently on her left hip to make her sit straight. The hand or a light rod can be used to tap the dog, but praise must be given with the correction.

If the crooked sit is in the opposite direction, reach back with your right foot and gently tap the dog's right hip to make her straighten out.

Both Heels And Sits Wide

With the dog on leash, walk her close to a wall or a fence. If she heels wide and bumps into the barrier, she may correct herself of this habit, especially if you encourage her to come close by patting your leg. If she veers away and won't be coaxed to sit close, avoid jerking the leash. Hold it tight and pull her to you, then tell her "Sit!" Wide heeling and sitting are usually the result of jerking the leash without adequate praise. They also result from grabbing at the dog while heeling, or from stepping into the dog when you halt.

Refuses To Sit And Stay

Put your dog on a long line and ask an assistant to hold the end of the line, some distance in back of the dog, or tie it to a stationary object. After you tell your dog "Stay," face her. Watch her carefully. Then kneel down, which may tempt her to break. If she does, call out from the distance, "STAY!" after which the assistant gives one jerk on the leash. Take the dog back and try again. This time you may have to clap your hands to get her to move. Try playing with another dog. The important thing is to tempt your dog to move so you can call out "STAY," from the distance, before the line checks her.

THE COME FORE AND THE GO-TO-HEEL POSITION
(The Finish)

While heeling your dog, walk backward and say, "Robin, come fore," "Come front," or just plain "Come!" When she turns to face you, bring her close by holding both hands under her chin and pulling the leash toward you. Give praise at the same time. After she comes close, command "Sit!" Then pat her. If she isn't sitting straight, square her up before you pat her.

With the dog now sitting facing you, say "Robin, heel," and walk past her to your right. Give the leash a tug as you go by, pat your side, and after the dog turns around, halt. Then pat her.

Next, to make the go-to-heel position easier, get the dog on her feet after you give the command. Bring her in front in the usual way by walking backward and telling her "Come!" After she is sitting in front, tell her "Robin, heel!" Then pull her to a standing position by taking two steps backward. After she is on her feet, take two steps forward to make her turn around. When you step back, pull on the leash and give praise. When you step forward, pat your knee to encourage her to turn around.

Next, pretend the right foot is glued to the floor or fastened to the ground. Only the left foot moves. After you say "Robin, heel!" take a big step backward with your left foot and guide the dog around to your left side with your left hand. Hold your hand under her chin. Take a big step forward with the same foot, as you pat your left leg to coax the dog to face front. Move the right foot only when necessary.

55

Try for a quick response to your command. After you give the command, snap the leash hard, give praise, then pat your side for encouragement. If your dog moves around to your side when she hears the command "Heel" or sees the hand move, don't jerk the leash but give praise as usual. The praise will help bring her around.

If you prefer to train your dog to go to the right and around in back, follow the same procedure in reverse. Give the command first. Follow by using the leash and giving praise for encouragement.

Teach your dog to go to heel position on signal. With the dog on leash, sitting facing you, hold the leash in your right hand. Drop your left hand as a signal to go to the left side. After you drop your hand, reach for the leash with the same hand and bring the dog around. Do this often enough and your dog will start for your left side when your hand starts to move.

Note: in Obedience Trials a dog is permitted to go to heel position by going to the right and in back of the handler. For the purpose of teaching, the left-side method of going to heel position will be used.

FINISH Problems—How To Overcome Them

Sloppy Finishes

In practice, hold the handle of the leash wadded into a ball, in your left hand. Do a series of:

1) Steps to the right
2) Quarter-turn pivots to the left
3) About-turns from a standstill
4) A step to the rear

With each change of direction, command "Heel!" Then snap the leash to make the dog assume the correct heel position. Give praise when you jerk the leash.

Ignores Command To Go To Heel

Put the dog on leash. Without moving your hands or your feet, command "Heel!" Then, if you are training a large dog, with BOTH hands jerk the leash to your left side and as far back as you can reach. Give praise and pat your knee to turn the dog and make her face front. When training a small dog, lean over so your hands are level with the dog. Use only the left hand to jerk the leash, and do it more gently.

In stubborn cases, an assistant can stand in back of and to one side of the dog (depending on which way she goes to heel) and, after the owner gives the command, the assistant gently taps the dog on the hip with his shoe, to make her start. The owner's praise and the patting of the leg encourage the dog the rest of the way.

Doesn't Do A Complete Finish

Put the dog on leash. Wad the handle of the leash into a ball and hold it in your left hand with elbow straight. Give the command "Robin, heel!" without moving your arm. As the dog moves around to the left side, wait and see if she does an incomplete finish. If she sits at an angle, jerk the leash just as she sits down, to make her move further around. It is important that you give praise after the heel command. Praise encourages a dog to do a complete finish. Praise softens the correction in case the dog sits crooked and you have to correct her.

COMING WHEN CALLED
(The Recall)

Start by teaching your dog to respond to the word "come." With the dog on leash, let her wander at will. When she is sniffing some object, or stands gazing off into the distance, call her name. Tell her "Come," and after you say it, snap the leash once, then clap your hands to encourage her to run to you. Do this until your dog will turn toward you, regardless of what she is doing, when she hears the word "come."

Next, leave her on a sit-stay. Face her the length of the leash. Say her name and tell her "Come!" Use a HAPPY tone of voice. **After** you call her (not **when**), tug on the leash to start her, then clap your hands and praise her while she is coming. After she comes, tell her "Sit," then pat her. Insist upon square sits and as close as possible.

Your dog may start toward you when you call, but then decide to go elsewhere. Change your voice to a demanding "COME!" Follow with one good tug on the leash at the point the dog veers away. The double command of "Come! Come!" is very effective when followed by a leash correction as the dog starts to amble off.

When you take the leash off, use the same HAPPY tone of voice. Follow the command with praise. Even clap your hands enthusiastically until your dog comes willingly. If she wanders off or runs away instead, use the demanding "COME!" If necessary, throw the leash at her heels to make her listen, then kneel and coax her to come. If your dog persists in running away, ask members of your family, and friends, to chase the dog back to you when you call. It is hard, by yourself, to correct a dog that runs wild.

After your dog is dependable, prepare her for the recall as it is done in Obedience Trials. Stand erect when you call her. Make her sit squarely in front after she comes. Have her complete the exercise by going to heel position on command or signal.

RECALL Problems—How To Overcome Them

Doesn't Come On First Command

Ask someone to stand directly in back of your dog. Get the dog's attention, then call her. Follow by clapping your hands and giving praise. If the dog doesn't start, the assistant lightly taps the dog's hindquarters with the toe of his shoe. Clapping the hands will make the dog forget the correction.

Tossing something lightly behind the dog from a hidden source will have the same effect, but take care the dog doesn't see the object thrown nor the person who throws it. Praise and the clapping of the hands will again overcome the correction.

Comes Before She Is Called

Leave your dog. Face her the length of the training area. Hold the rolled-up leash in your hand. If the dog starts before she is called, toss the leash in front to block her. Take her back and try again. In practice, alternate the come with the sit-stay.

Doesn't Sit Close On Recall

At the point where your dog slows down or comes to a sitting position, quietly but firmly repeat "Come, COME, COME!" until she moves forward to sit closer in front. When she does, reward her with a pat or, if she likes to eat, a tasty morsel. To bring the dog closer, use only your voice. Don't move your feet.

Doesn't Do A Complete Finish After She Comes

Put the dog on leash. Wad the leash into a ball and hold it in your left hand. Give the heel command without moving your arm. Let the dog move around to heel position and wait for her to sit at an angle. When she does, jerk the leash backward to make her move further around. Praise when you jerk the leash.

RECALL Problems—How To Overcome Them

Comes Slowly When Called

After you call your dog, turn and RUN. She should instinctively speed up. If she doesn't, ask an assistant to hide where the dog can't see him. When the dog slows to a walk or stops entirely, the assistant drops something in back of the dog to make her run toward the owner. The owner softens the correction by clapping his hands and giving praise, to assure the dog the correction was all in fun.

A slow response on the "come" is usually the result of inadequate praise while training the dog. Until your dog learns to run to you willingly and quickly, give praise with every command. The praise can be dropped after your dog responds with eagerness.

Goes Directly To Heel After Recall

Put your dog on leash. Face her for the recall. Ask an assistant to stand behind you. Call your dog but don't use the leash to make her sit in front. Wait for her to go to heel without sitting. When she does, the assistant drops something directly in front of her. After the correction, gather up the leash, make her sit straight, then praise and pat her. Repeat the exercise but take care the assistant makes the correction ONLY if the dog goes directly to heel without stopping in front. You can make the correction by holding something in your left hand and dropping it in front of the dog.

Crooked Sit On Come

With your dog on leash and sitting in front, hold the leash in BOTH hands. Tell her "Come!" Walk backward and take the dog with you. Halt, wait for the dog to sit at an angle, then pull the leash taut and spank her on whichever hip is out of line. Use either hand. Keep in mind that the dog should start to sit crooked before you correct her, and never correct her without giving praise.

Alternate correction: with the dog on leash, ask two assistants to stand two to three feet apart, and facing one another. Take your position on the third side of the square, facing the dog. After the dog comes, and if she starts to sit crooked, the slightest movement on the part of either assistant should make the dog correct herself and sit straight.

RECALL Problems—How To Overcome Them

Follows Handler When Left For The Recall Exercise

Carry some object in your left hand. This can be a rolled-up magazine or the leash wadded into a ball. After you leave your dog, if she follows, throw the object backward so it lands in front to block her.

Alternate method: after you leave your dog, turn and face her. Slowly walk backward. If she starts to follow, throw your leash in front of her, then take her back and try again.

LYING DOWN ON COMMAND OR SIGNAL

Keep these two things in mind when you teach your dog to lie down: (1) move slowly, and (2) give continuous praise while you ease the dog into the down position. If she struggles, don't force her. Hold firm until she relaxes, then continue with gentle training. You may have to out-wait your dog ten or fifteen minutes until she decides she will be more comfortable in a prone position than in the one in which you are holding her.

If it is a large dog you are training, face her and play the leash out until it touches the floor. Step over it with your right foot, so it will slide under your instep. When you do this, say "Stay!" (You don't want your dog to take a foot signal.) Take your foot away, then step over the leash again, repeating the word "Stay!" After the dog is sitting quietly, grasp the leash low down with both hands, say "Down," and slowly pull up, giving praise.

Do the same with a small dog, but when you pull up on the leash with the left hand, press on the dog's shoulders with the right hand. At the same time, scratch her shoulders and give praise. (See illustration.)

After your dog lies down on command, teach her to lie down on signal. With the dog on leash, face her (rather close). Put the leash on the ground and stand on it with your left foot (see illustration). Raise your right hand and tell her "Down!" Hold your hand with fingers pointing up while you step on the leash under the dog's chin

Teaching a large stubborn dog to lie down

with your right foot to make her lie down. Praise when you do it. The raised hand in the form of a salute is a signal easily seen at a distance. It is also a signal the dog won't confuse with any other signal. (Lowering the hand as a signal to down, for instance, is similar to the hand motion used when teaching the come, and your dog could be confused.) Use the same signal for a small dog but while teaching her to obey a signal, give it from a crouched position so the hand will be at the eye level of the dog.

Strive for a quick response to your command or signal to lie down. Hold the leash in your left hand, this time just clearing the floor. Raise your right hand and command "Down!" After you give the command, stamp on the leash with your right foot to get immediate action. When working with a small breed or a dog that is sensitive by nature, tap the leash gently. Give praise when you do it. If you are left-handed, follow the same procedure, substituting left for right and right for left.

Some dogs get stubborn when told to lie down. Others resent the command and will leap at the owner. In this case, hold the leash with about six inches dangling free. If the dog lunges forward or refuses to go down, flip the leash once across the tip of her nose, then pull up on the leash until she goes down. When you use the leash, be careful of the eyes. (See illustration.)

Teaching the signal for the DOWN

Hand signal DOWN from the side

Hand signal DOWN from the front.

When teaching your dog to lie down, the important thing is **not to jerk** her to the ground but to ease her to the down position, praising her while you do it.

Teaching a small dog the DOWN

THE DOWN-AT-HEEL POSITION

If you are training your dog for the Novice work in Obedience Trials, the down-at-heel position will prepare your dog for the long down exercise. If you are just a pet owner, you will use the down-at-heel on numerous occasions around the home.

To train your dog to lie down at your left side, place your left hand on the leash, close to the dog's collar. Kneel on your left knee, command "Down," and pull down. While you apply pressure on the collar, give praise. After the dog goes down, say "Stay!" Step on the leash with your left foot to keep the dog down, then stand erect. Give the command "Sit," tug upward on the leash, and after the dog is sitting, pat her. Putting a large dog down this way is safer than reaching over the dog's back, which brings a dog's teeth close to the trainer's face.

Do the same with a small dog but reach in front of your body with the right hand and apply gentle pressure to the shoulders while you pull down on the leash. Hold the small dog close to your body and she will feel secure.

THE DOWN-STAY
(The Long Down)

Now that your dog knows how to lie down, teach her to stay in the down position. With your dog in the down position, directly in front of you, back slowly away. If she gets up without permission, grab the leash quickly and put her down again. After the correction, back away slowly to see if she stays in the down position.

With a small dog, stand over her in a crouched position. Hold both hands close to, but not touching her. If she starts to get up, push her down quickly and tell her "Stay!" After she relaxes, back slowly away.

Circle your dog while she is lying down. Move slowly and if she tries to get up, tap her lightly on the nose or pull down on the leash to make her stay down. Tell her more firmly, "STAY!"

When you leave your dog in the down position when she is at your left side, signal the stay with the left hand and step out on the right foot. When you face her, hold both hands with palms toward the dog's muzzle and with fingers pointing down. If the dog starts toward you, block her and make her back up.

With your dog in the down-stay position, face her and gently pull the leash taut. If the dog uses the tight leash as an excuse to move forward, correct her by putting her down again and telling her in a more severe tone, "STAY!"

72

DOWN Problems—How To Overcome Them

Ignores Command Or Signal To Lie Down

Put the dog on leash. If it is a large dog, step over the leash with your right foot so it will slide under your instep. Hold the center of the leash in your left hand and the handle in your right hand with about six inches dangling. After you give the command and raise your right hand, flip the end of the leash once against the dog's muzzle. (Be careful of the eyes.) Then pull up on the leash and make the dog lie down.

With a small dog, lean over and after you raise your hand and give the command, bump the dog's nose once with the palm of your hand. After you bump it, press on her shoulders to make her lie down. Pat her!

Dog Creeps On The Down

Give the signal for the down by raising either hand, depending upon whether you are right- or left-handed. Hold your fingers pointing up. If the dog creeps forward, drop your hand quickly and tap her on the nose to make her draw back. After she draws back, pat her. With the small dog, lean over before you give the command or signal so your hand will be close to the dog.

Dog Sits Up When Handler Returns After The Long Down

When you return to your dog and find her sitting, or if she gets up while you are circling, drop your hand quickly and tap her nose. Tell her "DOWN!" After she is lying down, pat her.

Dog Is Slow To Obey The Signal And Command To Lie Down When At Heel Position

Put the dog on leash. Signal the down with the LEFT hand by holding the hand above the leash with wrist bent. Command "Down!" If the dog ignores the command and signal or is slow to obey, snap the dog to a down position by dropping the hand forcefully onto the leash.

DOWN Problems—How To Overcome Them

Dog Rolls Over When Told To Lie Down

After your dog goes down on command or signal, quickly call out "STAY!" Do this before she has a chance to roll over.

Creeps Forward When Made To Sit From The Down

After you give the command or the signal to sit, if the dog moves forward, lift your knee and bump her chest.

With a small dog, use the inside of either foot to bump her and make her draw back.

Dog Sits Up On The Down

Fasten her leash to a ring in the floor or in the ground, with the leash slack enough so the dog can start to get up but can't get to a sitting position. In time, she may correct herself. Try fastening a long line to her collar, then running it through a ring in the ground. You can make a sharper correction by giving a good tug on the line. When the leash is off, ask an assistant to stand close to the dog and tap her on the nose when she lifts herself to a sitting position.

Hand signal STAND from the side

THE STAND

With your dog sitting at heel position, wad the leash into a ball and hold it in your right hand. Place your right hand in front of your dog's muzzle. Reach over the dog's back with the left hand and while you tickle her stomach, pull the leash forward with the right hand, to make her stand. Tell her "Stand!" If she attempts to walk forward, bump her nose gently with the right hand—the hand that is holding the leash. A bump on the nose is effective and it won't make your dog hand-shy.

Next, teach your dog to stand on command while walking at heel position. Hold the leash in your right hand, and before you come to a halt, drop your right hand in front of the dog, tell her "Stand," and at the same time, reach over her back and scratch her stomach. Praise when you do this. Repeat the heeling and the standing-at-heel until the dog will stand by herself when you place your right hand in front of her. By giving the signal to stand with your right hand, you won't confuse the dog with the signal for the stays, where the left hand is used.

Teach your dog to resist pressure. Scratch her back. Push on it. She should brace her feet and stiffen her body. If she sits instead, tap her to a standing position and repeat the command more demandingly. When working with a small dog, loop the handle end of the leash under the dog's stomach to keep her standing.

The leash under the stomach works with large dogs as well as small.

THE STAND FOR EXAMINATION

At Obedience Trials, the judge examines each dog individually. Prepare your dog for this test by asking members of your family and strangers to examine the dog during the stand-stay. If she creeps forward, reprimand her sharply by tapping her under the muzzle. Bounce her to a standing position if she sits. If she moves because she is shy or because she is over-friendly, make her pay the consequences for ignoring your command to remain where left. A sharp correction from you will be effective.

The easy way to teach the STAND signal.

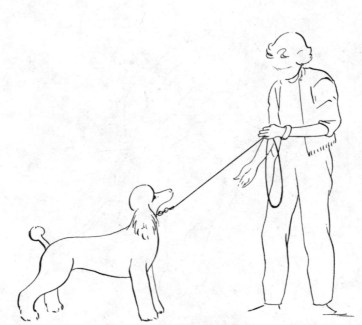

To overcome creeping, pull the leash taut. If the dog moves, tap her under the chin.

THE STAND-STAY

With your dog standing at heel, give the command and signal to stay. If your dog moves forward, correct by reaching backward and bumping her nose with the LEFT hand. If she sits, cuff her from underneath with the same hand.

When your dog will hold the stand, face her and try to pull her from the stand-stay position. When you draw the leash forward, she should brace all feet and refuse to move. If she moves, correct her! Tap her under the muzzle to make her back up, then repeat the stay command.

Circle your dog several times while she is standing. Return to heel by going to the right and around in back. Hold the leash to your left and keep it slack. If the dog moves forward or sits before you give permission, repeat the command in a demanding voice and correct rather sharply.

When you face your dog, hold the palms of both hands toward her muzzle with fingers pointing DOWN.

THE SIT, THE STAND, THE DOWN-AT-HEEL POSITION

Teach your dog the difference between sitting, standing, and lying down at heel position. When you halt, the dog should sit without being told. If she doesn't, spank her to a sitting position or use the leash with a backward snap. The important thing is to have your feet together before you make the correction.

To make her lie down, place your left hand on the leash close to her neck. Command "Down," and pull her head slowly to the ground. Praise when you pull down on the leash.

If you want your dog to stand, while still moving forward, drop your right hand in front of her and say "Stand," and at the same time stroke her back with the left hand or scratch her stomach to keep her standing.

STAND Problems—How To Overcome Them

Won't Stand At Heel

After you loop the leash under your dog's stomach, hold the center of the leash in your left hand (see illustration). While walking, signal the stand with your right hand. Don't pull up on the leash until the dog starts to sit down. Give praise when you lift her to a standing position. If you have a small dog, lift her gently.

Won't Stand For Examination

Loop the handle of a second leash around your dog's stomach. Ask an assistant to stand behind the dog and hold the handle of the leash, but to keep the leash slack. After you tell the dog "Stay," face her. If she tries to sit during the examination or moves forward, call out a second "Stay," after which the assistant should lift her to a standing position or pull backward to keep her from walking forward. The important thing is to call out the command before the assistant takes action.

Dog Shies Away From The Judge

Hold a rolled-up magazine in your hand during the examination. When the dog moves away from the judge, drop the magazine directly in front of her and tell her more firmly, "Stay!" If the judge comes in on the other side, and the dog shies in the opposite direction, drop the magazine there. The point is to block the dog in whichever direction she moves.

Dog Sits When Judge Examines Her

Have your dog straddle some object. For a small dog, this can be an empty coffee can. For the large dog, place a broom handle on the rungs of two chairs. Ask the "judge" to press on the dog's back lightly, forcing her to touch the object with her stomach. This should teach her to stiffen her legs and resist pressure while she is being examined.

STAND Problems—How To Overcome Them

Dog Growls And Snaps During Stand For Examination

Muzzle the dog and then ask three or four people to circle her, all at the same time, without touching her. Later, ask them, one at a time, to stroke her back and give praise. If she shows resentment, tell her in your most demanding voice, "STAY!"

Still later, hold a rolled-up magazine in your hand. If the dog growls, snaps, or moves away, drop the magazine directly in front of her and again tell her "No! Stay!" To make such a dog stay, the dog must be more afraid of the consequences for disobeying the owner's command, than of the judge who examines her.

Dog Sits As Handler Returns After Stand For Examination

After the dog has been examined, return to heel position, wait a few moments, then tell her "Stay," and leave her again. When you return to heel, avoid gathering up the leash, as this may tempt her to sit. When you pat her after the exercise is over, pat her while she is standing.

STICK JUMPING

Stick jumping is a change from the basic routine and dogs enjoy it. It teaches them to jump onto the grooming table, to leap in and out of cars and over small hurdles. It prepares them for advanced training, which includes jumping obstacles.

A sawed-off broom handle or a piece of dowling thirty inches long, will serve as a jumping stick. Hold the stick in your right hand. Wad the handle end of the leash into a ball and carry it in your left hand. Place the end of the stick against a stationary object, such as a tree or a post, but keep it LOW. The dog will eventually jump the equal of one and a half times her shoulder height, but while she is learning, hold the stick only a few inches above the ground and keep all hurdles low to the ground.

Give the jumping command, which can be "Over," "Hup," or "Jump," then pull the leash over the stick, ahead of the dog. While she is jumping, tell her "Good girl!" If she braces all four feet and refuses to jump, lay the stick on the floor or the ground, then slowly drag her over the stick, giving praise while you do it. If you allow your dog to balk at a jump, she will form a habit that is hard to break.

Next, teach the dog the jumping command. After she learns to jump freely, place the stick in front of her, command "Jump," and after you say it, give the leash a forward snap. While you are snapping the leash, give praise. It is important that you say the word "jump" before you tug on the leash.

When you take the leash off, after you place the stick, point to it with your left hand when you tell your dog to jump.

Stick Jumping

GENERAL Problems—How To Overcome Them

Dog Takes Judge's Commands

In practice, have someone call out the judge's command. Count five before you tell your dog what to do.

If you train by yourself, give the judge's commands aloud before you give the commands to the dog. This will teach your dog not to respond to the sound of the voice but to wait for definite words.

Dog Runs Away During Training

If your dog darts away while heeling, reach out and slap her across the rump to make her look around. If it is a small dog, drop something at her heels. Repeat the heel command, using a more demanding tone. Follow by patting your side and giving praise.

If the dog ignores your command to "come" and runs playfully about, throw something at her heels when she isn't looking, then drop to a kneeling position, call her and offer protection.

Teaching a dog to go to the person who calls, should be a family affair. At home and in the training area, cooperate by pointing to the person who called the dog and telling her "GO!" Chase her if necessary. To correct the dog that won't come when called, station one or two assistants in different parts of the training area, and arm them with an empty carton or two. When the dog ignores the command to "come," ask those who are assisting, to block the dog by dropping the carton in front of her, in order to drive her back to the person who called. In the meantime, the one who called the dog should kneel, clap his hands, give praise and offer the dog protection.

Anticipates Commands

Avoid following a set routine. For instance, alternate the come with the sit-stay. If your dog anticipates the "finish," pivot back on your left foot to heel position and don't let her complete the exercise. Each time she moves without permission, tell her "Stay" more emphatically.

GENERAL Problems—How To Overcome Them

Dog Whines During Sit- And Down-Stays

The following suggestions may lessen the whining, but may not be a complete cure:

Train your dog to stay alone, as much as possible.

Muzzle the dog temporarily, with a piece of gauze bandage. When she is quiet, take the bandage off. When she whines, put it on.

Consult your veterinarian. Ask if he recommends a tranquilizer to calm your dog's nerves.

Finally, buy a little water gun. Squirt water at her from the distance, every time she starts to whine.

A dog that has learned to stay alone will be less inclined to whine or to break on the stays than the dog that always has company. Train your dog to be independent so she will feel secure when you leave her.

Dog Loses Points For Sniffing

Make it a rule never to let your dog put her nose to the ground unless you give her permission. When she is on leash, whether she is walking, sitting, or standing, jerk up on the leash when the head goes down. When you enter the show grounds, be unusually strict about this. If you want her to exercise, give her a command such as "duties," or release her with an "O.K."

Dog Is Inattentive

In practice, turn unexpectedly during the heeling exercise or spank your dog playfully when she looks away. When you want her to come, don't wait for her to look at you before you call her. Give the command, then tug on the leash, whether she is looking at you or not. If she looks away during the stand, the sit, or the down-stays, yell "Hey," when she turns her head away. Use food to entice her if she is a dog that likes to eat.

GRADUATION

Requirements for receiving a diploma after a nine or ten weeks' training course: *

Dog to heel on a slack leash and to be under control at all times. Dog to sit automatically when handler halts.

Dog to stay for one minute in the sitting position, without a second command. Handler approximately fifteen feet away.

Dog to stay for one minute in the down position, without a second command. Handler approximately fifteen feet away.

Dog to hold the stand-stay position, without a second command. Handler holds the leash in his hand.

Dog to heel; alternate the sit-at-heel with the down-at-heel and stand-at-heel positions.

Dog to respond to the down, the come, and the "finish" (going to heel position) when both command and signal are used.

Dog to heel with leash over the handler's shoulder. Possibly, for the final test, the leash removed.

* Note: these are not the requirements for the Novice Class at an AKC licensed Obedience Trial but suggested requirements after a nine or ten weeks' training class.

Heeling and Sitting	Stays List Breaks			Sitting Lying down Standing at Heel	Quick Response to			Heeling Leash over Shoulder	Stick Jumping	Free Heeling	Remarks for Special Handling Award
List good workers	Sit	Stand	Down	List good workers	Down	Come	Finish	List good workers	List good workers	List good workers	
1				1				1		1	
					2	2	2				2 very difficult dog good handling
3	3		3					3		3	
4				4	4	4	4	4	4	4	
5		5		5	5	5	5	5	5	5	5 good handling dog no problem
6	6			6	6			6	6	6	

Best Performance

Prize	First	Second	Third	Fourth
Dog. No.	4	5	6	1

Handling Award

Dog No. 2

Note: When a number appears in every column except the Sit, the Down and the Stand Stays, the dog should not be overlooked for placement among the winners.

Sample judging chart for a group graduation

SUGGESTIONS FOR
EXHIBITING IN THE NOVICE OBEDIENCE CLASSES

Give your dog sufficient training, so you will feel confident when you enter the Obedience ring.

Read the Obedience "rule book" * carefully and familiarize yourself with the show ring procedure. The extra commands and signals, and body gestures you used to train your dog, are not permitted in a regular trial. Carelessness in handling could cause your dog to fail. When the rules do not forbid the second command, give an extra one if necessary and take a penalty. Permissible corrections at shows will keep a dog from getting ringwise.

In practice, train your dog in unfamiliar surroundings. When she gets to the show, she will be less distracted.

When you enter the show grounds, keep your dog from sniffing. Every time she lowers her head, jerk up on the leash to make her pay attention. Sniffing is a major problem of Obedience exhibitors.

The majority of dogs are at their best when they have been left alone, prior to competing. Staying by herself for only a few moments may alert your dog, and make her anxious to please.

Exercise and give your dog a drink of water before your turn comes

* *Regulations and Standards for Obedience Trials* available from:
  The American Kennel Club, 51 Madison Ave., New York, N.Y.
  The Canadian Kennel Club, 667 Yonge St., Toronto 5, Canada.
  Obedience rules are revised occasionally. Make certain you have the latest copy.

to enter the ring. If the dog is to do her best work, she must fee comfortable. Groom her for appearances' sake!

Take time and observe the judging procedure for the day. A judg usually follows the same pattern for each exhibitor. If, while working you fail to hear a command, you will have some idea of where to go because you watched the routine.

When you are in the Obedience ring, walk briskly and move in straight line. Keep your corners square and when you do an about turn, pivot smoothly, without fancy footwork. Some handlers take step backward before they turn, and this leaves the dog behind.

When the judge calls for a "FAST," change to a running pace Don't just walk a little faster. In the SLOW, avoid sauntering or you dog will want to sit down. When it is time for the Figure 8, take you position, facing the judge. If the judge wants you to go a certain way he will tell you. If not, select whichever way you please. While doing the Figure 8, walk naturally and let the dog change pace.

In the Obedience ring, THE STAND FOR EXAMINATION is don off lead. The leash is removed, and given to the steward. After you stand your dog, either by posing her or by giving a command or signal stand erect yourself, then automatically give the command and signa to stay, and leave her.

When you leave your dog for THE RECALL, go where the judge tells you, but avoid standing with your back against the rope or bar rier, or close to objects such as the judge's table or chair. Carelessnes in selecting a place to stand can cause your dog to do an incomplet "finish." When you give the command to "come," keep your voic HAPPY. If there is a great deal of noise, yell the command loude than usual.

During the LONG SIT and LONG DOWN exercises, place your arm band and leash far enough away so your dog won't be tempted to snif them. If it is the LONG SIT, have your dog sitting squarely on bot hips. If it is the LONG DOWN, leave her resting comfortably on on hip. Note that you cannot use your hands to position or down you dog. Give the command and signal together, but don't use your dog' your right foot from an upright position. Crouching encourages dog to follow.

While you are away from your dog, don't fidget. Your dog may in terpret the slightest body or hand motion as a signal to come.

When you return to your dog after the sit- or down-stays, take car not to step on her or bump her accidentally. By the same token, be considerate of your competitor's dog.

In practice, train your dog to lie down at heel position when you give a signal with your left hand. This looks well in the ring and if you have an excitable dog to handle, you can keep her under control more easily between exercises.

After your dog's performance in the Obedience ring, if you are pleased with the way she worked, don't be ashamed to show it. If you aren't pleased, let the ringside think you are anyway! Obedience is a sporting game, not to be taken too seriously.

BE PROUD OF YOUR TRAINED DOG.
MAKE HER A CREDIT TO OBEDIENCE.

BOOK TWO

OPEN
OBEDIENCE COURSE

CONTENTS FOR BOOK TWO
OPEN OBEDIENCE COURSE

OPEN CLASS EQUIPMENT

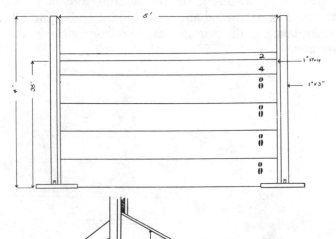

The Solid Hurdle. Detailed specifications may be found in The American and Canadian Kennel Club rule books for Obedience Trials.

The High Jump: Five feet wide. Adjustable in heights of from eight to thirty-six inches. Consists of four 1″ x 8″ boards, one 1″ x 4″ board and two 4-foot Standard uprights, each with a wide base, constructed with grooves into which the boards fit. (See **Regulations and Standards for Obedience Trials,** available from: The American Kennel Club, 51 Madison Ave., New York, N.Y. 10010 and The Canadian Kennel Club, 667 Yonge Street, Toronto, Canada.)

Note: One 1″ x 2″ board may be necessary to meet certain height requirements.

3

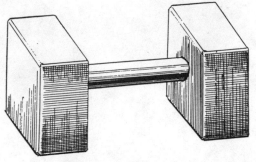

Paint it a light color.

The Dumbbell: Available in small, medium, and large sizes. Select a dumbbell made of hardwood and with square ends. End pieces should be sufficiently large to discourage the dog from picking the dumbbell up the wrong way.

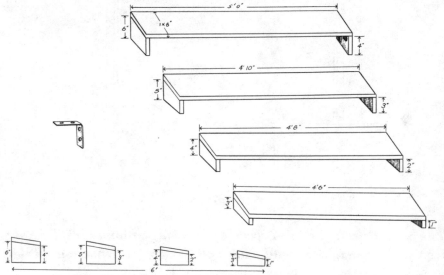

The Broad Jump. Drawings and detailed specifications may be found in the rule books.

The Broad Jump: Consists of two to four separate hurdles, five feet long and 8 inches wide, measuring 1 inch to 6 inches in height and adjustable from 16 inches to 72 inches in overall length. The flat surface of each hurdle slopes, allowing for a 2 inch difference in height between the front and the back edge of each hurdle. The hurdles are constructed in such a way that they telescope for convenient storage. (See **Regulations and Standards for Obedience Trials.**)

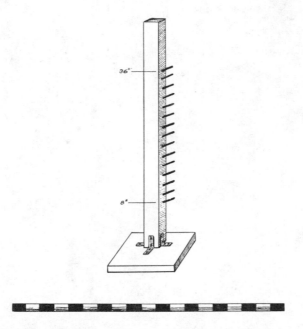

*The Bar Hurdle. This is not part of the Open
Course but is used for the jumping exercises.*

The Bar Jump: The Bar Jump is not part of the OPEN CLASS
equipment, but it will be used in the JUMPING exercise. Construction
is similar to that of the High Jump. Instead of boards, a square 2 to
2½″ wooden horizontal bar is used, which is adjustable for raising or
lowering according to the height of the dog. Adjustable for each 2
inches of height from 8 inches to 36 inches. (See **Regulations and
Standards for Obedience Trials.**)

Miscellaneous Training Equipment:

Training collar and a six-foot flat leather leash.

A long line with a snap on one end.

A small, rolled magazine.

A light rod, approximately 4 feet long (for clearing the High
Jump.)

A piece of chicken wire or hardware cloth, the size of the Broad
Jump.

TRAINING SUGGESTIONS

Plan your dog's schooling so training for the OPEN CLASS will be a series of progressive lessons. Long, long before you start the OPEN work, condition your dog for advanced training by encouraging her, while she is young (yes, even as a puppy), to carry assorted articles, to retrieve thrown objects and to leap small hurdles. If your older dog is just starting her Obedience career, include carrying and jumping as part of her Novice work. Owners can pave the way for the OPEN and UTILITY Classes without affecting a dog's performance while still competing in the Novice Class.

Timing is important! When you teach voice commands, give the command. Follow with the correction and praise.

When you teach hand signals, give the signal. Follow with the correction and praise.

When you want your dog to heel or to come, use her name with the command.

When you want the dog to perform at a distance, stress the command or give a signal without the name.

Give a command or signal ONCE. Repeat when necessary but put a correction with it.

Praise AFTER commands and signals and WITH corrections. The praise must be discontinued when exhibiting in Obedience Trials, but when used during the training period, your dog will be more responsive.

When you praise, BE SINCERE! Dogs respond to a cajoling tone of voice.

Modify your method of training to the SIZE AND TEMPERAMENT of the dog. Not all dogs train alike!

When you correct, disguise corrections so you and your assistant will not appear responsible.

If you inadvertently make a harsh correction or misjudge the timing, make up to your dog immediately; then be careful not to repeat the mistake.

If you find that one of the suggested corrective methods has a bad effect on **your** dog, don't use it. Dogs react differently to corrections.

When problems come up, work backward. If your dog won't retrieve over the hurdle, lower the jump until she gains confidence. If she won't **retrieve on flat,** go back to the HOLDING and "TAKE IT!" exercises. Praise and a fresh start have a magical effect when a dog is temporarily confused.

If you use your hand at any time to reprimand your dog (such as cuffing the dog's nose for creeping), pat her with the SAME hand you used to correct her. Your dog must think the hand correction was accidental.

Don't be surprised when you attempt to solve one problem if your dog slips back on some other part of the exercise. For instance, if you have been correcting your dog for NOT coming, she will undoubtedly come a few times TOO soon. The setback, while discouraging, is temporary, and in time you will balance the training.

A good trainer will never use food as the ONLY inducement for making a dog obedient, but if your slow performer peps up when you give food, use it to overcome problems.

If you are NOT successful in your training, BE MORE DEMANDING. Each time you correct for a REPEATED mistake, use a firmer tone of voice and jerk the leash harder.

Strive for perfection from the beginning. When you are careless about little things, they become problems later on.

The suggestions offered in **The Complete Open Obedience Course** will be more effective if your dog received the basic training outlined in **The Complete Novice Obedience Course.**

The instructions given in the succeeding sections of this book are for people who are right-handed. Those who are left-handed may follow the same instructions, simply substituting the left hand for the right, and the right hand for the left. However, in Obedience Trials a dog must heel on the handler's left side.

8

For the purpose of teaching, the OPEN class exercises are broken down to include:

Heeling

Drop In The Distance

Drop On Recall

Retrieve In Play

Holding On Command

Carrying On Command

Jumping

Jumping While Carrying

The "Take it!"

Reaching For The Dumbbell While Walking

Picking Up The Dumbbell From The Ground

Picking Up The Dumbbell On Command While Walking

Retrieve On Flat

Retrieve Over Hurdle

The Broad Jump

SIT- AND DOWN-STAYS (Handlers out of sight)

What may prove to be a difficult situation with one dog during training for the advanced work, will present no problem for another. By dividing the OPEN CLASS work into **exercises,** rather than weekly lessons, owners can select that part of the text instruction that applies to the needs of their dog.

HEELING

Heeling With Turns

Perfection in FREE HEELING is achieved through leash training. Study your dog's natural movements and select a speed suitable to the dog. The heeling exercises will then be a normal procedure, based on the dog's physical and mental characteristics. If you have not already done so, get into the habit of starting the heeling action with your LEFT foot. In the Novice work, it didn't matter which foot you started on, because the Novice exhibitor normally uses the heeling command. Then too, when working with a large untrained dog, the trainer has better balance when he starts on the right foot. For the advanced training, teach your dog that when your RIGHT foot moves, it means to STAY. When your LEFT foot steps forward, it means to FOLLOW.

A common mistake made by amateur trainers is to jerk the leash when they step forward at the start of the heeling exercise. This TIMING is incorrect! There should be no hand movement, only the verbal command, such as "Robin, Heel!" which is given before the foot moves. The leash is jerked AFTER the trainer starts, while the foot is coming down on the first step, and WHILE the trainer is giving praise. A gentle patting of the side follows EVERY jerk of the leash.

The majority of dogs perform with accuracy when the leash is on but will take advantage on the HEEL FREE. To overcome this independent attitude, surprise your dog by USING the leash when she doesn't expect it. During the heeling routine, turn sharply at short intervals and catch her off guard. AFTER you turn, tug on the leash forcefully, using a minimum of hand motion but with exaggerated praise. Do this two or three times, then make the turns WITHOUT jerking the leash but GIVE PRAISE JUST THE SAME. If the leash is used continuously, your dog will heel wider than ever, or will heel close through fear.

Practice about-turns from a standstill. As you pivot, reach back with your RIGHT foot and tap the dog lightly on the right flank. Bring your feet together, reach down and pat her immediately. The dog must think the foot correction was unintentional. But you accomplished your purpose by making her turn.

Make one complete circle to the right, first while in motion, and again from a stand. Circling keeps a dog alert and watchful of movements. If it is a big dog you are training, reach back with your right hand when you make an about-turn, and "spank" the dog playfully on the rear. When she looks around in surprise, clap your hands in front of your body and coax her to come close at heel. Encouraging your dog to remain at heel position through cleverly disguised tricks is a better method of training than jerking the collar repeatedly.

Fast And Slow

During the heeling exercise, dash forward and snap the leash **with praise.** Slow to a walk, and say a quiet "Good Girl!" Do a fast run **without** jerking the leash, but give praise just the same. The praise can be dropped after your dog has learned to change pace, but during the teaching stage, the dog will be more responsive if she thinks the jerk on the leash is part of a running game.

The Figure 8

Train your dog to do a close Figure 8 the same way you taught her to do the Fast and the Slow. Circle two posts, two chairs, or two of anything, placed approximately six feet apart. When your dog is on the outside of the circle, SPEED UP, jerk the leash with a series of snaps and give praise. When the dog is on the inside of the circle, slow to a walk, while you continue the praise. The third or fourth time you circle the "posts" with the dog on the outside, speed up without jerking the leash, and when the dog changes pace, praise her for doing so.

11

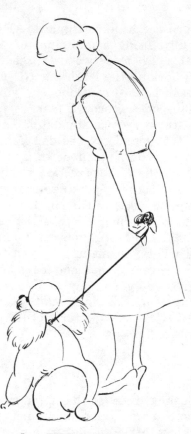

Bring your feet together BEFORE you correct for sitting ahead.

Sits

Wad the leash into a ball and hold it in your LEFT hand. Keep your elbow straight with your arm close to your body. Go through the heeling routine and make the necessary heeling corrections in a playful manner. When you halt, bring your feet together, WAIT, and see what happens. If your dog passes your knee, snap the leash backward with force to make her sit immediately. Give praise when you do it. If the dog stops when you stop, but continues to stand, or is slow to sit, transfer the leash to your right hand and, with the left, "spank" her to a sitting position, then follow with exaggerated patting with the SAME hand. Even a small dog will accept corrections cheerfully, working happily and with spirit, when corrections are made the right way.

Finishes

With the leash in your LEFT hand and your dog at heel position, hold your arm close to your side with elbow STRAIGHT. Command "Heel!" and take one step to the RIGHT. Give praise and jerk the leash IN BACK of your body to make the dog move with you.

Make a quarter turn to the LEFT. Pivot on your left foot, don't step! Say "Heel!" and snap the leash backward to make your dog square herself around to sit at the proper heel position. Don't forget the praise!

A series of BACKWARD steps will help teach your dog the correct heel position. Step back with your LEFT foot, command "Heel!" and snap the leash backward, again with praise. Before you realize it, your dog will automatically shift her position whenever you move away from her or when you turn your body.

Say "Stay!" and with the leash still in your LEFT hand, face your dog. Stand directly in front of her. Hold your left elbow STRAIGHT! Tell her "Robin, Heel!" then WAIT, for you must do one of three things: If the dog starts on command, praise her as she moves around to your left side, but don't move your arm. If she doesn't start on command, snap the leash past your side and give praise simultaneously. If she moves around to your side on command but does a sloppy finish, wait until she starts to sit, THEN jerk further back to make her do a more complete finish. Give praise when you use the leash.

If you have trained your dog to go to heel position by going to the RIGHT and around in back, make corrections with the RIGHT hand.

Practice the heeling exercises with the leash thrown loosely over your shoulder or tucked under your belt, and with your hands at your waist or at your side. Correct each mistake by snapping the leash sharply, then let go of it at once. Follow each correction with a gentle patting of your left side to encourage the dog.

FREE HEELING

When you take the leash off, remember the following:

Walk in a straight line. Angling into your dog will cause her to heel wide.
Walk briskly! Don't adapt your pace to that of the dog.
Hold your LEFT hand close to your body!
Give the first command in a happy tone of voice.
Change to a demanding tone or call your dog's name sharply if she lags or ambles away. AFTER the second command, gently pat your side and give praise.
If forging is your problem, or if your dog attempts to dart away, STAND STILL! Signal back with your left hand and repeat the heel command forcefully, then pat your side coaxingly.

When your dog is doing a good job of FREE HEELING, give her credit! Praise her while she is working. The praise can be discontinued AFTER THE DOG IS TRAINED, but while learning, every dog needs encouragement.

If you are training a large dog, carry the leash folded twice, with the snap end in your RIGHT hand. If the dog fails to pay attention, call her name loudly or reach out and "spank" her playfully on the hindquarters with the end of the leash, then coax her close by patting your side.

If all attempts to keep your dog at heel position fail, snap on the leash, give it ONE good jerk to bring the dog in close, and try again. The change in voice, followed by flattery, with the occasional use of the leash, should eventually teach your dog to stay at your side at all times. Especially if you make the heeling fun! On every halt, avoid stepping into your dog. The foot that is furthest back is brought forward to meet the foot in front. When the action is in reverse (toward the dog) the dog will draw away, fearful of being stepped on.

When teaching your dog FREE HEELING for the OPEN Course, the length of the practice sessions will vary, depending upon the dog. Short lessons with generous praise and patting, with the offering of a few tempting tid-bits, are generally effective. Far more important, by keeping the training a pleasant experience, you will have a HAPPY working dog!

14

HEELING Problems—How To Overcome Them

Forging

Leash corrections can be made by an assistant who walks at the dog's left, while holding the leash in the RIGHT hand. The owner commands "Heel!" When the dog forges, the assistant jerks backward on the leash while the owner gives praise.

For off-leash corrections, the assistant walks backward in front of the dog. After the owner gives the heel command, if the dog forges, the assistant tosses some object (an empty cardboard carton is excellent) directly in front of the dog, or bangs on the floor with a rolled magazine. These are excellent corrections for instructors to use with unruly dogs in a Beginner's Class. For proper timing, the owner must give the heel command before the instructor makes the correction.

Lagging And Heeling Wide

Lagging and wide heeling are difficult problems to overcome once they become a habit. There is no one magical cure. If your dog is the greedy type, carry food to encourage her to stay close. When you take the leash off, have a fishline or a strong piece of string already attached to the collar so you can make corrections when the dog doesn't expect them. If the dog is not the scary type, ask three or four assistants to help by dropping articles surreptitiously, and ONE AT A TIME; or to push some object, such as an empty carton or a folding chair, toward the dog when she lags or heels wide. Tapping the floor with a long pole in back of the dog is also effective. Be careful not to overdo corrections and be generous with praise.

Dog Lags On The Figure 8

Hold the leash in BOTH hands, low and close to your body. When the dog is on the INSIDE of the circle, walk naturally. When she is on the OUTSIDE, speed up, jerk the leash in a series of snaps, giving praise. About the third or fourth time around, speed up WITHOUT jerking the leash, but give praise just the same. This teaches your dog to change pace, an important feature of the

HEELING Problems—How To Overcome Them

Figure 8. When you take the leash off, walk naturally but continue with the praise until your dog consistently remains close.

Dog Is Slow To Sit On The Halt

Put the dog on leash. Wad the leash into a ball and hold it in your LEFT hand. Keep your elbow straight. AFTER your feet come together, jerk the leash backward with force to make the dog sit. The important thing is not to be moving your feet at the time you jerk the leash.

LARGE DOGS

An assistant at the dog's left can spank the dog to a sitting position AFTER the handler halts. Don't forget the praise.

SMALL DOGS

Carry a light rod in your RIGHT hand. The leash in your LEFT. After you halt, reach in back of your body and tap the dog gently, but firmly, on the hindquarters.

Dog Heels On Wrong Side

Reach back with your RIGHT hand and cuff the dog's nose when she comes in on your right side. After which, pat your left leg with your LEFT hand to encourage her to heel there.

Carry something in your RIGHT hand, firm but soft, that just clears the floor. Make the same correction. Or, kick back with your RIGHT foot when the dog comes in on the right.

Heavy-Set Dog Fails To Change Pace

Heel the dog between two people. When you run, give praise. If the dog doesn't run with you, the person on the dog's left jerks the leash forward, with BOTH hands. When the leash is off, continue giving praise when you change pace, until the dog thinks running is part of the game.

HEELING Problems—How To Overcome Them

Dog Bites At Hand

Hold the LEFT hand still. Slap the dog's nose with the RIGHT hand. At the same time, tell her "Stop it!"

Dog Lags And Is Wide On The Right-About-Turn

LARGE DOGS

"Spank" your dog when you make the turn. Reach back with your RIGHT hand or your RIGHT foot and tap the dog's hindquarters, then clap your hands playfully in front of your body, to encourage her to come close.

SMALL DOGS

Put your dog back on leash and make sharper corrections.

Dog Nips Ankle On The Fast

Ask an assistant to hold a small, rolled magazine or the leash wadded into a ball. When your dog barks or nips your ankle when you run, have the assistant throw what she is holding at the dog's feet and tell the dog "Stop that!" Give praise, especially when your dog will run without misbehaving.

Dog Sits Ahead

LARGE DOGS

The correction is the same as for slow sits. After you halt, jerk backward on the leash, held in the LEFT hand.

Or, have an assistant make the correction from the dog's left.

SMALL DOGS

Same, but in a more gentle manner, although the severity of the correction really depends upon the temperament of the dog.

Alternate correction: Bring the leash in back of your body and hold it in your RIGHT hand. After you halt, jerk the leash to the right. Give praise!

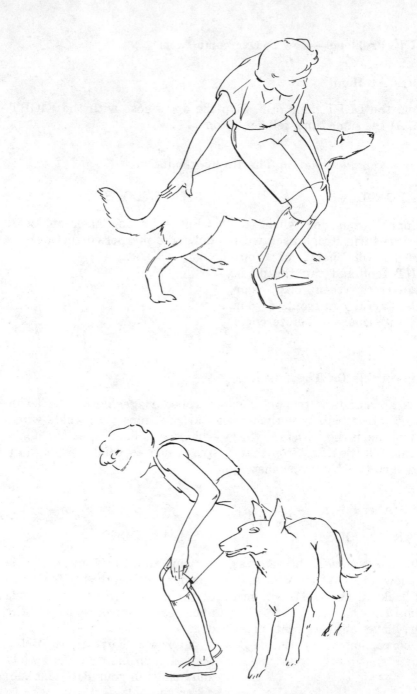

Playful corrections get excellent results.

Dog Sits At An Angle

Walk the dog between two people. If she swings her hindquarters AWAY from the handler, the person on the dog's left taps the dog on the hip to make her sit straight.

Same, but done gently with a light rod held in the RIGHT hand. Or, the assistant can use the heel of her right foot.

If the crooked sit is in the opposite direction, the handler reaches back with her RIGHT foot and taps the dog on the right hip to make her straighten the sit.

Dog Heels And Sits Wide

With the dog on leash, walk her close to a wall or a fence. If she goes wide and bumps into the barrier, she may correct herself, especially if you encourage her to stay close to your side. If she veers away when you halt, pull the leash tight WITHOUT JERKING IT, and hold her until she sits close.

Wide heeling is usually the result of jerking the leash without adequate praise. It also comes from grabbing for the dog while she is heeling free. Wide sits are the result of stepping into the dog on the halts.

DROP IN THE DISTANCE

Owners of Novice dogs would do well to postpone the DROP ON RECALL until their dogs have gained the C.D. degree. The "drop," which sometimes slows a dog up on the COME, could result in lower scores while the dog is competing in the Novice Classes. Practicing the DROP IN THE DISTANCE, however, alternating it with the COME, and the SIT and STAY, is good training experience for the dog.

Before you attempt to make your dog drop at a distance, teach her first to drop directly in front of you on the FIRST command and on the FIRST signal. With the dog on leash, facing you, hold the leash in your LEFT hand (it is presumed, of course, that your dog already knows how to lie down as outlined in **The Complete Novice Obedience Course**). WITHOUT MOVING YOUR BODY, command "Down!" Use a quiet tone of voice and follow the command with "Good Girl!" The praise is important! It encourages the dog to obey without leash correction. If one is necessary, it will be more favorably received. If your dog obeys the first command to lie down, go to YOUR right, circle around in back, and while she is in the down position, pat her. If the command is ignored, quickly stamp on the leash with your RIGHT foot to get her down, giving EXTRA praise. Circle around, pat her, but don't let her get up until you give her permission. With a small dog, or one that is extra sensitive, tap the leash more gently.

Certain dogs, especially Hounds and Toy breeds, resent the snap on the collar used to put a dog down. In this case, lean over so your hands are close to the dog. Give the command, and, if ignored, BUMP the palm of your hand ONCE against the dog's nose, PUSH her to a down position by pressing on her shoulders, then pat her or scratch her ear. The bump on the nose can be most effective when used the RIGHT way. The right way is with fingers pointing UP.

After your dog lies down on voice command, tell her "Sit!" This time raise your RIGHT hand (this is the signal used by right-handed people to make the dog lie down) and follow the signal with "Good Girl!" If your dog isn't down by the time your hand is raised with fingers pointing UP, stamp on the leash or bump the palm of the raised hand against the dog's nose, with EXTRA praise. Say "DOWN!" at the same time, then circle around to heel position and pat her while she is lying down. The important things to remember are these: Give the command WITHOUT BODY MOTION; when you use the signal, raise your hand, WAIT, then make the correction; and whether you use your hand or your foot to get your dog down, give PRAISE! The way you give the signal is also important. Lift your hand quickly, then lower it slowly while the dog is in the process of going down. If you drop the hand too fast, it will look like the signal to come and your dog could be confused.

When your dog will lie down immediately on a single command, and will do the same when you give the signal, try it without the leash, but stay close to your dog. Give the command or signal ONCE, then follow with praise. The praise can be dropped AFTER the dog has learned to react immediately, but during the teaching, praise should accompany the voice and the hand gesture. When the leash is off, and the command or signal is ignored, the bump on the nose is an effective correction. Return to heel position each time your dog goes down; pat her or give her a tasty morsel so she will associate something pleasant with the prone position.

Gradually increase the distance you stand away, but ONLY if your dog will drop immediately, on a single command or signal, a distance equal to the length of the leash. With the dog some distance away, the VOICE now becomes the correction. When the command or signal is ignored, give the second command demandingly.

The ultimate goal for the DROP IN THE DISTANCE should be twenty-five to thirty feet, to prepare your dog for DROP ON RECALL.

If you still have trouble making your dog lie down at a distance, fasten a long line to her collar and run the line through a ring in the floor, or one placed in the ground. Ask an assistant to hold the end of the line at a distance (or hold the line yourself). Tell your dog "Stay!" Face her, then give the signal or the command to lie down. If she remains sitting, the pull on the line will put her down. Return, make her sit, and repeat the exercise.

DROP ON RECALL

When your dog is ready for the DROP ON RECALL, put her back on leash and face her at its full length. Call her by name, command "Come!" then follow with "Down! Good Girl!" Don't let the dog get up too much speed before you drop her. Give the command without bending your body, and DON'T YELL! If the training for DROP IN THE DISTANCE has been adequate, you should have little trouble with the DROP ON RECALL exercise. However, if your dog continues toward you after you give the command (and you had better be prepared for this), run forward, bump her nose gently with the palm of your hand, using a backhand motion (like that used when playing tennis), making the correction with as little hand motion as possible. After the dog lies down, pat her.

Practice a series of "drops." Call your dog, run backward, and, without leaning forward, tell her "Down!" After she is down, call her, run backward, and drop her again. Do this first by command and then by signal, following each drop with praise. Try the exercise off leash. Keep your body upright. Use the same calm voice you used when the leash was on, and give the same type of signal. If you yell or make frantic motions, your dog may think she has done something wrong and will try to dart away.

The distance you stand from your dog is gradually increased. She should also be made to drop at various distances from the spot where she is called. If you make your dog lie down in the SAME spot each

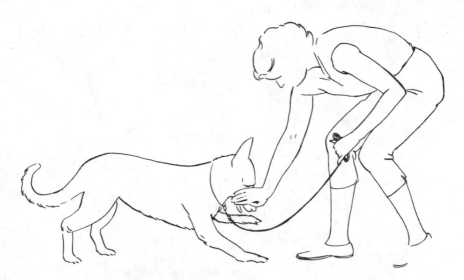

Used the RIGHT way, a bump on the nose stops creeping.

time, she will very likely anticipate the command and drop before she is told.

In practice, alternate the DROP ON RECALL with a straight RE-CALL and with the DROP IN THE DISTANCE. This will teach your dog to wait for commands, and not to act when she hears your voice. When training, give the command quietly. Signal the drop without too much violence.

DROP ON RECALL failures can usually be traced to yelling at the dog, thus frightening her, and to excessive body motion, which is confusing.

Things To Remember When Teaching DROP IN THE DISTANCE And The DROP ON RECALL

Keep the dog on leash.

Teach your dog to drop directly in front of you before you make her drop at a distance.

Without bending forward, tell your dog to drop (command or signal).

When you use a voice command, avoid yelling.

Train your dog to drop when you RAISE your hand.

If the dog doesn't obey the FIRST command or signal, bump her nose with the palm of your hand, or stamp on the leash forcefully. At the same time, say "DOWN!" and after the dog is down, pat her!

When you take the leash off, increase the distance you stand from the dog—but **not** if you have to tell her twice before she obeys.

When the command or signal is ignored at a distance, call out demandingly, "DOWN!" then **run** forward and make the necessary correction.

While the dog is learning, give praise WITH every command and WITH every signal.

After your dog knows the DROP ON RECALL, alternate with the straight RECALL, and with the DROP IN THE DISTANCE.

Dog Does Not Come On First Command

Ask someone to stand close to your dog. Get the dog's attention, then call her, and follow the command with praise. If she doesn't start, the assistant taps the dog on the rear with the toe of her shoe as though it were accidental. After she does it, clap your hands playfully, and give extra praise.

Tossing something at the dog from a hidden location will have the same effect; but take care that the dog does not see the object thrown or the person who threw it. Cover up every correction with play.

Dog Comes Before She Is Called

Leave your dog. Face her at the length of the training area. Hold something in your hand. If the dog starts before she is called, toss what you are holding in front to block her. Take her back and try again. In practice, alternate the come with the sit-stay.

Dog Is Slow To Drop On Command

With your dog on leash, face her at its full length. Call her and run BACKWARD. Before she catches up with you, and while you are still backing up, give a quiet command "Down!" then run FORWARD and bump the dog's nose gently with the palm of your hand. Use a backhand motion like that used when playing tennis, with fingers pointing UP. When the dog is down, praise and pat her.

Dog Is Slow To Drop On Signal

With your dog on leash, face her at its full length. Call her, run BACKWARD, and while still backing up, raise your hand, which is the signal to go down; then run FORWARD and bump the dog on the nose gently, with the palm of the SAME hand. Again, keep the fingers pointing UP! Pat the dog after she lies down.

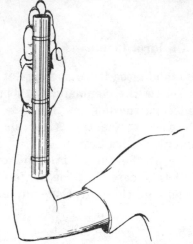

When you use corrective tools, disguise them.

Dog Continues Forward After Given Signal To Drop

Leave your dog, and face her at a distance. Hold a small, rolled magazine (taped in the center and on each end) along the palm and wrist of the hand you use to give the signal. Call your dog signal the drop, and, if she obeys, say a quiet "Good Girl!" Complete the exercise the usual way. If she ignores the signal, toss the magazine directly in front of her, and while your hand is still raised, command "Down!" When she obeys, go to her, pat her, or give her something to eat as a reward.

Dog Comes Slowly When Called

After you call your dog, if she slows up, turn and RUN, or turn your back and clap your hands. Your dog should instinctively speed up. After she comes, if she likes to eat, give her food.

An assistant can toss a small object in back of the dog if the dog doesn't know he is there. Five things are important: (1) Do not let the dog see the object when it is thrown. (2) Give praise with the correction. (3) Throw the object only when necessary. (4) After the correction, run, clap your hands and make a game of the training. (5) Reward the dog when she comes, using food if necessary

DROP ON RECALL Problems—How To Overcome Them

The line is effective with large dogs as well as small.

Dog Continues Forward After Commanded To Drop

Same as for not dropping on signal, EXCEPT that the magazine is tossed underhanded. Don't throw the magazine unless the dog ignores the command, and give praise with the correction. The leash rolled into a ball can be used the same way. The object is to check the dog's forward movement after the command has been ignored.

Alternate correction: Fasten the dog on a long line, equal in length to the distance the dog must travel BEFORE you drop her. Tie the other end of the line to a stationary object in back of the dog. Call her, then signal the down BEFORE she reaches the end of the line. When the line checks her, tell her "Down!" again, then go to her, and praise and pat her.

Note: When making a correction for DROP ON RECALL, there should be a pause between the giving of the command or signal and the throwing of an object. If the line is used to make the correction, the command or signal should be given BEFORE the dog reaches the end of the line. This is to give the dog a chance to obey before she is corrected for disobedience. Improper timing will cause a dog to fear the drop and look cowed.

27

DROP ON RECALL Problems—How To Overcome Them

Dog Anticipates Drop

Same as for coming slowly, but after the correction, call the dog straight without making her drop.

Dog Doesn't Come In A Straight Line And Veers To The Side On The Drop

Form a narrow aisle with two lines of people facing each other. As the dog passes down the center and is made to drop, ask your assistants to reassure the dog with quiet praise. Widen the aisle gradually.

Dog Stops On Signal But Remains Standing

Put your dog on leash, stand her, then ask an assistant to stand at the dog's side, with leash in hand. Tell your dog "Stay!" Face her some distance away, then give the command or signal to lie down. If the dog ignores it, the assistant makes the dog go down by pulling up on the leash, sliding it under her foot. Make the dog stand and repeat the lesson until she will lie down immediately on command or signal, from a standing position. With small dogs, the pull on the leash is gentle.

Alternate correction: Use the line through a ring in the floor or the ground, and practice pulling your dog down from a standing position.

Dog Anticipates Come After Drop

Call your dog. Drop her! After she drops, turn and walk away. If she starts to follow, DEMAND "STAY!" Return after a few moments, face her, and call her or go back to her and pat her while she is still lying down.

Practice calling another dog's name AFTER your dog has dropped. If your dog comes, call out "Down! Stay!" Let her learn to wait for HER name.

In practice, alternate the DROP ON RECALL with the DROP IN THE DISTANCE, and with the SIT-STAY exercises. This will teach your dog to wait for COMMANDS, not to act out a definite routine.

RETRIEVE IN PLAY

Teach your dog to carry while she is young.

As suggested earlier, holding, carrying, and retrieving do not have to be associated entirely with a dog's adult life, or with Obedience Trials. Even a young puppy can be taught to hold and carry if you place something in her mouth and encourage her with "Take it to so-and-so!" Carrying from one person to another thus becomes a game, and with it, comes a chance to show off. These early attempts at carrying will teach your dog, with a minimum of effort, the basic steps of the RETRIEVE exercise, one of the most difficult in advanced training.

If your dog is a natural retriever, take advantage! Make a game of retrieving objects, both in the house and out-of-doors. Concentrate on getting your dog excited so she will chase things, then just before she reaches the object, give the retrieve command ONCE. **While she is picking up the object,** say "Good Girl!" and say it as though you meant it. Praise will encourage a dog to take things from the floor or the ground when she might otherwise refuse.

If your dog starts for an object and comes back without it, or if she doesn't start at all, run to the object, pick it up, scuff it between her paws in a teasing manner, drag it along the floor, or kick it around; then place it in her mouth (unless she reaches for it herself), and turn and run. If she follows, clap your hands, squeal with delight, but DON'T REACH FOR WHAT SHE IS HOLDING. Let her strut around proudly, then, after a few moments, call her, quietly take the object away, and throw it again. If she won't give you the article when you say "Out!" cuff her gently on the nose with your free hand, and after she lets go, tell her "Good Girl!" and pat her.

Make your dog understand that after every retrieve she must bring the article back to you. For best results, kneel when you call her and give praise in a happy, high-pitched tone. If she starts running around with the article, change to a demanding "COME!" (throw your shoe or the leash at her if necessary) then coax her to come close by tapping the floor or the ground. When she comes, pat her before you take the article so she will learn to expect a pleasant reward for delivering things.

Train your dog to retrieve playfully while on leash. This will prepare her for leash corrections, which later may be necessary. While you hold the handle of the leash, make a game of throwing objects, letting the dog run after them. When she picks them up, don't forget the praise! If she sniffs the object, then walks away, kick it around like you would a football. Kick it first away from her, then toward her paws. Talk to her at the same time in a cajoling tone of voice to give encouragement. If she still won't pick it up, hand it to her, then try again.

RETRIEVE IN PLAY lessons should be short so your dog won't get tired of the game. You fail in your objective if the dog gets bored and refuses to pick up thrown articles in play. Another thing—don't always make your dog sit after she picks up the article. The steadying-down process required for Obedience Trials can be applied AFTER the dog has learned to retrieve on command. For the play training, keep things exciting.

When practicing RETRIEVE IN PLAY, use an assortment of articles for your games, and among them include the dumbbell. The retrieve exercise should not be associated with any one object. It is also important that you give the retrieve command just before your dog reaches for the article and that you praise enthusiastically while she is picking it up. Afterward, quietly but firmly insist that she bring the article to you.

Things To Remember When Teaching The RETRIEVE IN PLAY

Play games every chance you have.

Use an assortment of articles, and include the dumbbell.

Practice RETRIEVE IN PLAY, both on and off leash.

Keep the retrieve command a happy one.

Give the command ONCE.

Give praise while your dog is taking the article from the floor or the ground.

Allow your dog to chase articles without waiting for them to stop rolling.

Don't insist that the dog sit every time she returns.

When you take the object from your dog, never pull on it.

As the dog progresses, delay the praise until she is on her way back WITH the article.

Train often, but keep the lessons short.

If your dog has no interest in playing games, give her straight obedience. Owners with little previous experience can successfully teach their dogs to retrieve on command by following the instructions outlined on the following pages, but take ONE step at a time, and thoroughly master it before going on to the next!

HOLDING ON COMMAND

If you have taught your dog by playful means to **hold** what you give her, you can pass up this part of the training. The older dog that doesn't know what it means to carry things around will require the gentle, FIRM instructions outlined in this section.

The first lesson is to teach your dog to HOLD your finger. This isn't as dangerous as it sounds, because even a strange dog will seldom bite when handled in the proper manner. With your dog on leash and sitting at your left side, stretch the leash taut and step on it with your RIGHT foot. This will keep the dog from backing away. Gently place your LEFT hand around the dog's muzzle (unless it is a short-nosed breed, in which case, hold the skin on the side of the neck), and hook the little finger of your RIGHT hand under the collar beneath the dog's chin. By pulling the collar FORWARD, you apply pressure to the back of the neck, which keeps the dog from getting out of hand.

Place a finger or thumb very gently into the dog's mouth, holding it directly behind the canine teeth. When you do this, say "Take it Good girl!" Press the jaws together, still giving praise, to keep the dog from mouthing your finger. When she holds without struggling command "Out!" and take your finger away. Do this several times then use an assortment of articles, including the dumbbell. MOVE SLOWLY! HANDLE QUIETLY! Don't forget the PRAISE!

32

The first HOLDING lesson. Holding your finger!

When you work with the dumbbell, keep your hands close to the dog.

Teach your dog to grip things securely! Take one end of the object and SHAKE it gently while it is in her mouth. If she tries to give it to you, tell her "Hold it! Hold it!" and don't permit her to let go until you command "OUT!"

Some dogs, no matter how calmly they are handled, become hysterical and fight desperately the first time an object is placed in their mouths. In this case, tighten your grip, momentarily, by pulling the collar FORWARD and UP. This brings pressure on the back of the dog's neck and lifts the front paws off the floor so the dog can't keep her balance. By clamping the jaws together and forcing her to hold what you give her, the struggle should cease immediately. Having won the battle, calmly lower the dog's feet to the floor, pat her, scratch her ear, then remove the object. (It is suggested that you use some object other than your finger for this part of the training.)

When your dog will hold an object without spitting it out, scratch her ear with one hand, but KEEP THE OTHER HAND UNDER THE DOG'S CHIN! If she lowers her head as though to drop the article, cuff her chin up, and tell her "Hold it! Hold it!" If she drops what she is holding, the correction is one sharp tug on the leash, a tap on the nose, and telling her "Phooey!" BEFORE you pick the article up from the floor to make her try again.

Practice the SIT-STAY exercise while your dog holds different articles, among them the dumbbell. Practice the RECALL while she carries them to you. After you call, TURN and walk away. This will teach your dog to carry while heeling, which she should do if you give the heeling command, or encourage her by saying enthusiastically "Let's go!" When you halt, give a quiet "Sit-stay!" to keep the dumbbell in her mouth.

When teaching HOLDING ON COMMAND, avoid long training sessions. Five or ten minutes at a time is sufficiently long, and your dog won't get tired or become bored with the dumbbell work. Avoid training in extreme heat. Dogs perspire by panting. When the mouth must be open to breathe freely, the dog won't grip the object firmly

Things To Remember When Teaching HOLDING ON COMMAND

Keep the dog on leash.

Flatter your dog while she is holding. Scratch her ear, stroke her head. This will take her mind off the desire to drop the article.

Hold your hands close to the dog while she is learning. Move quickly if you think she is going to drop what she is holding.

If the head goes down, tap your dog under the chin and say "Hold it! Hold it!"

Shake the article lightly while it is in the dog's mouth so she will learn to grip securely.

Keep lessons short.

Don't train when the weather is hot.

Don't train when the dog is panting from excitement.

Practice with articles made of wood, metal, leather and other material.

While your dog is holding, get her to a standing position by tickling her under the stomach.

Keep her standing by scratching her ear and giving praise.

If she decides to trot around, clap your hands, turn your back and walk away. Give extra praise.

When you pat your dog, keep your hands away from the head. Pat her on the rear instead.

Whenever she drops what she is holding, shame her, then correct with a tap on the nose or a tug on the collar, BEFORE you pick the article from the floor to try again.

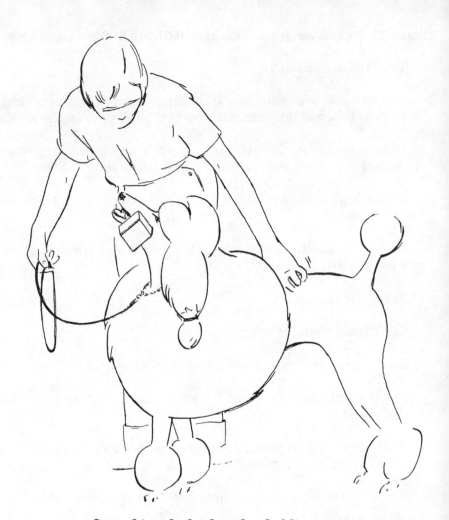

Scratching the back makes holding easier.

When you take things from the dog, see that she lets go when you tell her. If she doesn't, cuff her nose ONCE with the free hand, or blow in her face. When she releases the article, praise her.

After your dog learns HOLDING ON COMMAND, hand her things whenever you have a chance. Insist upon obedience. Praise and pat her when she keeps things in her mouth. Correct her sharply when she drops things without permission. When she becomes dependable, she is ready for the next step, CARRYING ON COMMAND.

CARRYING ON COMMAND

If your dog will hold what you give her, either as the result of early puppy training or the methods described in HOLDING ON COMMAND, teach your dog to carry while on leash. Dogs often carry things by themselves but will drop what they are holding when the leash is on. Give your dog something to hold, then scratch her back or tickle her stomach to get her to a standing position. KEEP THE LEASH SLACK, and, if she has not yet dropped the article, turn your back, run, clap your hands (this has a magical effect), and say "Let's go!" Use a cajoling voice when you praise; and when you pat your dog, keep your hands away from the object she is carrying. Pat the hindquarters, not the head.

If your dog refuses to walk while holding, coax her! Tap the floor, and give praise in a high-pitched voice. If she decides she has nothing to fear, and will take a few steps toward you, stand up, TURN AND WALK AWAY. See if she will follow. The important thing is to keep the leash slack. The choking effect of a tight collar will cause a dog to drop what she is carrying.

A small dog will get accustomed to a forward motion while holding, if you pick her up and carry her a few steps. Gradually lower her to the floor, then stand behind her, and PUSH her gently from the rear. The habit of "freezing" when an article is placed in the mouth, can be overcome by quiet handling with generous praise.

Don't be surprised if your dog keeps dropping things you give her, and when she does, don't become impatient or annoyed. This is a crucial point in your dog's obedience career. It is better to take extra time to accomplish your objective than to make the dog dislike the carrying exercise because you are overly anxious.

Carry the small dog!

Push from the rear!

Things To Remember When Teaching CARRYING ON COMMAND

Train your dog, while she is young, to carry all sorts of articles.

When the dog is holding, and the leash is on, KEEP THE LEASH SLACK.

If your dog refuses to walk while carrying, coax her by tapping the floor, or push her gently from the rear. Scratch her back, tickle her stomach, but, most important of all, talk to her in "baby talk."

If your dog will hold the object, TURN AWAY, CLAP YOUR HANDS, and make a game of the carrying.

If she still hasn't dropped what she is holding, run with her in play.

Give praise in a high-pitched tone of voice. Dogs respond to cajolery.

If your dog keeps dropping the article through sheer stubbornness, be more firm with each correction without losing your temper or becoming impatient.

Praising and hand clapping work magic!

JUMPING
(The HUP!-HEEL Exercise)

Your dog may be a long way yet from retrieving, but why not brighten the training routine by teaching the JUMPING exercise? Place the Solid, the Bar, and the Broad Jumps in different parts of the training area. Keep the Hurdle and Bar Jumps LOW, and the Broad Jump NARROW. The jumps can be raised or widened after your dog has become an expert at leaping obstacles, but to simplify the training and make proper corrections, it is important that the jumping be ridiculously easy the first few times.

With your dog on leash, hold the leash in BOTH hands, as when teaching the heeling exercises. Approach the Bar and the Hurdle Jumps slowly, and STEP OVER with your dog. Keep the leash sufficiently taut so the dog can't dart off to one side. If she balks at the hurdle, **pull** her gently over, WITH PRAISE! If she ducks under the bar, cuff her nose to make her draw back, then encourage her to go over the top. When approaching the Broad Jump, speed up a little, and leap over WITH the dog.

The JUMPING command may be "Jump!" "Over!" or "Hup!" and should be given BEFORE the leash is used to pull the dog across. Avoid a lifting motion. Use a forward thrust that will not throw the dog off balance, and give praise while the dog is jumping. After she lands, command "Heel!" and jerk backward on the leash, PAT YOUR SIDE, and encourage the dog to walk at heel position. The important thing to keep in mind when teaching the JUMPING exercise is NEVER let your dog refuse a jump once you have given her the jumping command. Make her go over, even if you have to lower the jump almost to the floor, or tip the individual boards of the BROAD Jump on their sides. Refusing a jump, thus getting her way, will encourage her to balk whenever she feels like it.

When your dog is familiar with the different types of hurdles, and will leap them on command, it will no longer be necessary to step over with the dog. Walk past the hurdles instead, and meet her on the other side. While the dog is jumping, hold your LEFT arm away from your body so the leash extends STRAIGHT UP FROM THE CENTER OF THE HURDLE. While the dog is landing, drop your left arm, so as not to throw her off balance when she lands. After she jumps, slow down or come to a standstill, and command "Heel!" Snap backward on the leash, **pat your side,** and give praise.

When your dog will jump and stay at heel without corrections, try the JUMPING exercise without leash. Approach each hurdle in a fast walk, POINT TO IT WITH YOUR LEFT HAND, and give the jumping command. Pass by the hurdle quickly, slow down, command "Heel!" and signal backward and pat your side. Don't run when teaching JUMPING. Running gets a dog excited and causes confusion. As a result, you may inadvertently make a bad correction that could affect your dog's jumping career.

Whether schooling a dog for Obedience competition, or for fun and exercise, the accepted height of a jump for most breeds is one and one-half times the height your dog measures at the withers (this is from the top of the shoulder to the floor). Current Obedience Regulations provide the following exceptions:

> The jump shall be once the height of the dog at the withers, or 36 inches, whichever is less, for the following breeds: Bloodhounds, Bullmastiffs, Great Danes, Great Pyrenees, Mastiffs, Newfoundlands, St. Bernards. The jump shall be once the height of the dog at the withers, or 8 inches, whichever is greater, for the following breeds: Clumber Spaniels, Sussex Spaniels, Basset Hounds, Dachshunds, Cardigan Welsh Corgis, Pembroke Welsh Corgis, Australian Terriers, Cairn Terriers, Dandie Dinmont Terriers, Norwich Terriers, Scottish Terriers, Sealyham Terriers, Skye Terriers, West Highland White Terriers, Maltese, Pekingese, Bulldogs, French Bulldogs.

The Broad Jump is twice as wide as the height of the High Jump. For instance, if your dog measures 16 inches at the shoulder, she should jump 24 inches in height and 48 inches in length. Don't expect your dog to jump exaggerated distances. In her efforts to please, she could have a bad fall, or she may learn to climb the hurdle instead of clearing it, which, in Trials, counts as a penalty.

RECALL OVER THREE HURDLES

A cuff on the nose will teach your dog NOT to go under the bar.

As your dog progresses in the JUMPING exercise, set the three jumps in a row, approximately fifteen feet apart. This is a fun-exercise that is enjoyed by both dogs and owners. Place the Broad Jump on one side of the Solid Hurdle and the Bar Jump on the other. With your dog on leash, leave her on a sit-stay in front of a NARROW Broad Jump. Face her on the opposite side. Tell her "Jump!" then snap the leash toward you with praise. Tell her to sit, then pat her.

Lead her to the LOW Solid Hurdle. Tell her "Stay!" and face her from the opposite side. Stress the JUMPING command when you call her. After she jumps, make her sit, pat her, then move on to the Bar. The Bar Jump, too, must be absurdly LOW.

When your dog is reliable and will jump all three hurdles on leash, try them with the leash off. Use the command "Come!" and then encourage the dog to leap each hurdle by calling loudly "Jump!" "Hup!" or "Over!" Try one jump at a time until your dog knows this part of the exercise, then try two hurdles. Leave her in front of the Broad Jump while you go to the opposite side of the Solid Hurdle. Call her, and if she jumps the two, lead her to the Bar, and make her jump that. If she starts around the jumps at any time, run forward and block her, then coax her to come over the top.

After sufficient practice, try all three. Leave the dog sitting in front of the Broad Jump. Face her from the far side of the Bar Hurdle. Kneel, then call her. As she approaches each of the three hurdles, call out a loud jumping command, and follow each command with praise. The Bar Jump will be the most difficult of the three, unless you have taught your dog STICK JUMPING and she is familiar with a single bar. Stand close to the last jump, and be ready to block her from going around the end or from ducking under the bar. If she attempts either, cuff her nose gently with the back of your hand, then pat the top of the bar and encourage her to come over the top. With practice, your dog will soon learn to leap all three hurdles on command, a useful exercise for exhibition work.

Owners who have trouble with their dogs running around the hurdles in this exercise should ask six people to assist, one standing at each side of the three hurdles. If there are not enough assistants available, chairs or other objects can be used. The fact that someone is standing in the way or that some obstacle blocks each side of the jumps, will encourage the dog to leap over the top instead of running around the ends.

An alternate method is for an assistant to hold the dog's leash when she is left sitting in front of the Broad Jump. The owner, from in front of the Bar Jump, calls the dog while the assistant runs with the dog and guides her over each hurdle. Timing the command with the correction is important. The owner calls out the jumping command as the dog approaches each hurdle. The assistant tugs on the leash if the dog starts around the end.

Things To Remember When Teaching JUMPING

Teach your dog to jump obstacles of various shapes and sizes.

Keep the dog on leash until she knows how to jump.

Keep the jumps simple during the first few lessons.

During the "Hup! Heel!" exercise, leap the hurdles with your dog to give her confidence.

Give the jumping command BEFORE you use the leash to pull the dog across.

Move the leash over the jump AHEAD of the dog.

Give praise while the dog is jumping.

Never permit your dog to balk at a hurdle. If she does, pull her slowly across.

If your dog tries to duck under the bar, cuff her nose with the back of your hand to make her draw back, then coax her to jump by patting the top of the bar.

If she fears the bar, place the pole on the floor or the ground and WALK the dog back and forth several times, until she is no longer afraid.

During the "Hup! Heel!" exercise, after your dog jumps each hurdle, call out a loud "Heel!" and snap backward on the leash, then pat your side and keep your dog at heel position.

When practicing the RECALL OVER THE THREE JUMPS, kneel when you call your dog, stress the jumping command as your dog approaches each hurdle, and give praise while she is jumping.

JUMPING WHILE CARRYING

Having trained your dog to CARRY and to JUMP on command, JUMPING WHILE CARRYING should create no problem. Follow these suggestions:

While your dog is learning, keep the jumps simple.

Keep your dog on leash.

Hold the leash slack. A choking effect will cause your dog to drop what she is carrying.

Encourage your dog by stepping over the jumps with her.

Give praise while the dog is jumping.

If your dog balks at a hurdle, correct her for refusing to jump, but not while she is holding. Take away the object so she won't associate the correction with the **carrying**. Make the dog jump back and forth several times over the hurdle. Give the jumping command first, then snap the leash sharply, with praise. After which, lower the jump, give her the object to hold again, then coax her to leap over by patting the top of the jump or by tapping the floor on the opposite side.

Avoid running while teaching JUMPING WHILE CARRYING.

Keep your dog under control by making her walk at heel both before and after she jumps.

Having learned CARRYING ON COMMAND and JUMPING, your dog is now ready for the "TAKE IT!" exercise. This means reaching to take an object from the hand.

THE "TAKE IT!"

(Reaching On Command)

If your dog will reach for an object when you say "Take it!" the training outlined here will not be necessary. If the older dog has never learned to take things from your hand, or you have a dog that refuses to pick up an object because she is tired of playing games, put the dog on leash and make her sit at your LEFT side. Your dog must first reach to take things from your hand on command before she will reach to take things from the floor.

Slip the collar high behind the dog's ears, and keep it there by applying slight pressure with the LEFT hand. Hold the dumbbell, or whatever object you are using, in the RIGHT hand. When working with a small dog, squat or sit on the floor and you will be more comfortable. **Your command should include praise,** such as "Take it!— Good Girl!" Timing is of special importance. Hold the dumbbell close to the dog's muzzle and give a SINGLE command. Use a quiet tone of voice! While you are saying the "Good Girl!" tighten the collar slowly with the LEFT hand by pulling the leash UP and FORWARD. This brings the dog's head to the dumbbell. At the same time, pry open the dog's mouth with the middle finger of your RIGHT hand, slip in

The first lesson of "Take it!" Note how the middle finger pries open the dog's mouth.

Your dog must first take the dumbbell from your hand before she will take it from the ground.

the dumbbell, release the collar, then pat the dog. After she holds the dumbbell a few moments, command "Out!" and take the dumbbell away. While working, move slowly and handle calmly. Each time you tighten the collar, increase the amount of pressure slightly, until your dog will open her mouth automatically when she sees the dumbbell coming, or when you tell her "Take it!"

The steady tightening of the collar, used for the first few lessons of the "TAKE IT!" exercise, gradually changes to short, quick snaps. Hold the leash in your LEFT hand as usual. Place the dumbbell close to the dog's muzzle, and this time, while you are saying the "Good Girl!" give the leash a sharp tug. The severity with which the leash is jerked depends upon the size of the dog, her temperament, and upon the length of time the dog has been in training for this particular exercise. If too much force is applied early in the training, the dog's attitude will be one of defiance. You will have the problem of keeping the dog's spirits up, as well as teaching her the exercise.

Things to Remember When Teaching The TAKE IT Exercise

Place the dumbbell directly in front of the dog's muzzle and hold it steady.

Give the command in a quiet tone of voice.

Give the command ONCE.

Follow the command with praise.

While giving praise, apply slow pressure on the collar with the LEFT hand.

Alternate the steady tightening of the collar with a short snap of the leash, depending upon whichever gets results.

If your dog turns her head from the object you are holding, use your knee or your hands to block her and make her face front. Turning the head is usually the result of forcing things into the dog's mouth, instead of bringing the dog's head to the object held in the hand.

Avoid working for long periods at a time.

When you take things from your dog and she tightens her grip, cuff her nose ONCE with your free hand, take the object, then pat her.

In practice, use an assortment of articles, as well as the dumbbell.

Train your dog to take an object while she is in the down position.

Train her to take one from a standing position.

Keep in mind that **your dog must reach to take an object from your hand on command before she will reach to take it from the ground.**

When you master the "TAKE IT!" part of your dog's training, she is ready for REACHING FOR THE DUMBBELL WHILE WALKING, a grade **up** in the retrieving exercise.

REACHING FOR THE DUMBBELL WHILE WALKING

Having learned to reach for an object from a sitting, a standing and a lying-down position, REACHING FOR THE DUMBBELL WHILE WALKING will not be too difficult. Wad the leash into a ball and carry it in your LEFT hand. Hold the dumbbell in your RIGHT. WHILE WALKING, place the dumbbell close to your dog's muzzle, and give a quiet command of "Take it!" Follow with a series of short tugs on the leash with the LEFT hand, while you keep saying "Good Girl!" Continue walking until the dog takes the dumbbell, either because she reached for it, or because you slipped it in her mouth. When she is holding, come to a halt, or take the dumbbell while still in motion, and give the dog an extra pat with praise.

The instinct to chase a moving object may give your dog the necessary incentive to grab for the dumbbell, especially if you encourage her. If she does grab for it, lower the dumbbell a little each time, until she is almost taking it from the floor. If the urge to chase things is lacking, the series of tugs on the collar must be increasingly sharper, until the dog will reach on command to take things while in motion.

When working with a small dog, it is easier to practice from a kneeling or squatting position. By circling to your right, you can keep the dumbbell moving ahead of the dog with a minimum of effort. At

Reaching! A step forward in the Retrieve exercise.

the same time, the training is brought down to the eye-level of the dog.

For practice, walk backward while the dog follows, facing you. Hold the dumbbell in the RIGHT hand above the leash, which comes from under the dog's chin. As you back up, say "Take it!" then give a series of tugs on the collar with the left hand, with generous praise. If your dog reaches for the dumbbell, halt, make her sit, pat her, then take the dumbbell. If she still doesn't reach, pry open her mouth, slip the dumbbell in, halt, then pat her.

Whether working in a circle or walking forward, gradually lower the dumbbell until one end is almost touching the floor or the ground. Finally, drag one end **on** the ground.

Things To Remember When Teaching REACHING FOR THE DUMB-BELL WHILE WALKING

Keep moving the dumbbell slowly AWAY from the dog.

Give the command ONCE.

Follow the "Take it!" command with praise.

Apply pressure on the collar by tugging at the leash held in the LEFT hand.

Give praise when you tug on the leash.

If your dog clamps her jaws together and refuses to open her mouth, apply STEADY pressure by holding the collar taut. Slip the dumbbell into the dog's mouth, release the pressure, and give praise and a pat.

If response is slow, give a sharper tug on the collar.

When teaching your dog to HOLD, to CARRY, and to REACH for an object, be definite about your dog's training. When you give your dog something to hold, she should hold it until you take it away, providing it is a reasonable length of time. When you give her something to carry, she shouldn't drop it without permission. And when you tell her "Take it!" she should reach AT ONCE for what you tell her to take.

Perhaps you accomplished this training through play, and only minor corrections will be necessary. But if you failed your objective, be more demanding, so that you and your dog will make progress. After your dog learns to HOLD, to CARRY and to REACH on command, you can use RETRIEVE IN PLAY to get her to pick things up from the ground. Play combined with OBEDIENCE at this point keeps a dog happy. When dogs enjoy their work, results are more pleasing.

Encourage play retrieve but keep your dog on leash.

If there is no interest in games, owners should follow the procedure outlined in the next exercise, PICKING UP THE DUMBBELL FROM THE GROUND. Retrieving on command is a difficult exercise for amateur trainers to teach; but if they will take one step at a time, and thoroughly master it before going on to the next, even the most stubborn dog can be taught to retrieve on command. In time, the dog will actually enjoy this exercise.

PICKING UP THE DUMBBELL FROM THE GROUND

If you have not been successful in teaching RETRIEVE IN PLAY, put your dog on leash. Sit on the ground or on the floor, and hold the leash in your LEFT hand close to the dog's collar. Take the dumbbell in your RIGHT. Play with your dog in a teasing manner. Hide the dumbbell behind your back. Scuff it between the dog's paws. Get her interested so she will lower her head. When she does, WHISPER the command "Take it!" and tug on the leash ONCE while you say the "Good Girl!" Slip the dumbbell into her mouth, then pat her.

Do this several times, then drag one end of the dumbbell along the floor, and see if she will reach for it there. If she shows no interest, tap her paws lightly with the end of the dumbbell to make her look down, snap the collar ONCE, giving praise, then slip the dumbbell into her mouth. Try baiting by rolling the dumbbell along the floor, or tossing it at the dog's feet. Place the dumbbell on a low bench or table, and encourage her to "Take it!" from there. Each time your dog picks up the dumbbell, succeeding times will be easier. Remember the **single** command and the praise WHILE THE DOG IS REACHING.

Even though your dog retrieves in play, give her this systematic training so she will always be reliable. Otherwise, whenever she doesn't feel like retrieving, she will tell you, "Pick up the dumbbell yourself!" For best results, keep the dog on leash, avoid yelling the

Bring the training down to the dog's level!

command (a playful tone is more effective), and when you tug on the leash, give praise.

When your dog will reach to take an object from your hand, either through play or through leash training, "accidentally" drop the article, and see if your dog will reach to take it from the floor. If she does, show YOUR enthusiasm by clapping your hands and complimenting the dog with excited praise. If she ignores what you dropped, kick it around and see if that will arouse her interest. If not, there is little you can do except to pick up the object and hand it to the dog with a sharper correction.

Teaching a dog to pick up the dumbbell (or other objects) is a matter of repetition and applying a bit more force each time WITH PRAISE. Take care not to become impatient, and when the dog clamps her jaws together and defies you to open them (which she will), quietly but firmly apply pressure by holding the collar taut. At this point, the dog will swallow, or open her mouth to protest, and you can quietly slip in the dumbbell and pat her.

Things To Remember When Teaching PICKING UP THE DUMB-BELL FROM THE GROUND

Sit on the floor or the ground with your dog and be comfortable.

Attempt the exercise first as a playful game.

Keep your dog on leash.

Give a **single** command.

Follow the command with **one** tug on the leash, slip the dumbbell into the dog's mouth, then pat her.

Each time you use the leash, snap it a **little** harder.

Whether you use the leash or whether the dog picks the dumb-bell up by herself, give praise.

Try baiting! Scuff the dumbbell between your dog's paws. Draw it away in a teasing manner. Kick it with your foot.

Roll the dumbbell away from the dog. Toss it playfully at her feet.

Tap the dog's paws with one end of the dumbbell to arouse her interest.

Encourage her to take the dumbbell from the floor while she is lying down. Encourage her to "Take it!" from a low bench or table.

Train often, but not for long periods at a time.

If snapping the leash doesn't get results, try tightening the collar by using a steady pull.

When it is hot, or if your dog is excited and panting, postpone the dumbbell work until a cooler time of day, or until the dog has quieted down.

Use an assortment of articles for this exercise, not just the dumbbell.

When you have succeeded in getting your dog to pick up the dumbbell and other objects on a single command, either as the result of play or from systematic training, your dog is ready for Picking Up The Dumbbell On Command While Walking.

PICKING UP THE DUMBBELL ON COMMAND
WHILE WALKING

With your dog at heel position, hold the leash wadded into a ball in your LEFT hand. Carry the dumbbell in your right. Start walking, and toss the dumbbell to the floor or the ground a few feet ahead of your dog. Give the command "Take it! Good Girl!" walk slowly past the dumbbell **without moving your left arm, and without coming to a definite stop.** If the dog reaches for the dumbbell, keep the leash slack so you won't distract her by jerking her collar, and give extra praise while she is picking it up. If she passes the dumbbell WITH-OUT picking it up, jerk the leash BACKWARD once to check her forward movement, then repeat the command in a demanding voice. If she still doesn't reach for the dumbbell, pick it up and hand it to her; praise her, then try again.

The first command is given in a happy tone of voice, followed immediately with praise. As explained previously, praise overcomes uncertainty and encourages a dog to take things from the floor when she might otherwise refuse. More important, praise disguises corrections.

When you teach PICKING UP THE DUMBBELL ON COMMAND WHILE WALKING, it is vitally important that you do not move your left arm or lean forward with your body, until you see how your dog reacts. If she passes the dumbbell without picking it up, there is still time to jerk the leash backward as a checkrein, after which you must stop long enough to help the dog take the dumbbell.

56

It is equally important that praise follow every command. You will get quicker results with praise than you will with force, and your dog will respond more willingly.

For the PICKING UP THE DUMBBELL WHILE WALKING exercise, use an assortment of articles, so that picking up an object on command will not be associated only with the dumbbell. Learning to carry and to retrieve various articles also conditions your dog for the Utility Class training, which includes scent work with different articles.

Train your dog in strange locations, and don't be too quick to remove the leash. You may need it for that all-important correction. When your dog will automatically reach for a dropped object or will pick one up on a single command, whether standing or in motion, whether at home or in unfamiliar surroundings, you are ready to continue training for the RETRIEVE ON FLAT exercise.

Things To Remember When Teaching PICKING UP THE DUMBBELL ON COMMAND WHILE WALKING

Keep the dog on leash.

When you throw the dumbbell (or other article) in front of the dog, give a happy command and follow the command with praise.

Don't stop when you come to the dumbbell. Slow up but continue to walk past it.

Don't move your left arm until you see what the dog does.

Don't lean forward!

If your dog reaches for the dumbbell, keep the leash slack, and give extra praise.

If she walks past the dumbbell, jerk BACKWARD on the leash; then stop long enough to make her take it. At the same time, use a more demanding "TAKE THAT!" and apply pressure with the collar, either by snapping the leash or by pulling it taut.

Avoid jerking the leash while your dog is reaching for the dumbbell. A jerk at the wrong time could discourage her from future attempts at PICKING UP THE DUMBBELL WHILE WALKING.

57

RETRIEVE ON FLAT

With your dog on leash and sitting at your left, tell her "Stay!" and **place** the dumbbell on the floor directly in front, so the dog can reach it by lowering her head. Hold the leash in both hands, low down and close to your body. **Without moving your arms,** give the retrieve command and follow the command with praise, such as "Take it—Good Girl!" The praise may encourage your dog to reach for the dumbbell, and if she does, pat and praise her! If she ignores it, the correction is one downward snap on the leash, with extra praise, after which, slip the dumbbell into her mouth, then pat her. By giving the command without moving your body, you teach your dog to **start** on the first command.

Remember, flattery will encourage a dog to do something when she might otherwise be stubborn, so be generous with your praise while teaching your dog to retrieve on command. Praise is especially important when you apply pressure to the collar.

If you still can't get your dog to pick the dumbbell off the floor on the first command, try an alternate method. Hold the leash in both hands as described above, but lengthen the leash so that the loop that leads back to the dog's collar is four or five inches from the floor. Tell your dog, "Stay!" and place the dumbbell directly in front, then give the command without moving your body. If the dog starts, give praise. If she doesn't, quickly stamp on the leash with the **left** foot to

Give the command BEFORE you step on the leash.

jerk her head down, and pick up the dumbbell and hand it to her Timing in this exercise is of extreme importance. Give the command without body motion, and if there is no response, jerk the leash and give praise at the same time.

If your dog will pick up the dumbbell from directly in front, tell her "Stay!" and place it at arm's length. The important thing is to have the dumbbell close enough that you WON'T HAVE TO MOVE YOUR FEET when you make a correction, yet far enough away that the dog must make an effort to "go" for the dumbbell. Give the retrieve command in a normal tone of voice, and follow the command with praise. If the dog starts, fine! That is just what you want her to do. If she doesn't, snap the leash sharply toward the dumbbell, using either your hands or your left foot, and give praise when you do it. Follow by picking up the dumbbell and handing it to the dog.

When your dog will retrieve the dumbbell the length of the leash on a single command, throw it even further. Give the command, let the dog start, then run with her toward the dumbbell. When she picks it up, run backward, then encourage her to bring it to you and to sit in front. Square all crooked sits, and insist that the dog perform as perfectly as possible on the finish. Carelessness in little things creates problems later on.

By this time, your dog may think retrieving is a game. In this case, take the leash off, and hold the collar so the dog can't start until you tell her. Throw the dumbbell, and just as the dumbbell stops rolling, release her and whisper the retrieve command. The dog should dart off immediately, and if she does, don't forget the praise while she is picking it up. If she decides to chew the dumbbell, or to run around with it after she gets it, kneel, give a forceful "COME!" and follow the command with "Good Girl!" Keep demanding "Come!" and at the same time coax her by tapping the floor or the ground; but don't run after her. If necessary, turn and walk away. Then, if she comes, pat her and make her sit; take the dumbbell, and after doing so, make her go to heel position.

If your dog starts for the dumbbell on command, then comes back without it, run forward and block her. Jerk her collar once, or kick the dumbbell toward her feet, and say "TAKE THAT!" in a demanding voice. After she takes it, run backward, and encourage her to come to you and sit in front. If you think she is going to drop the dumbbell (as many dogs do), be one jump ahead of her. Tap her under the chin and say "Hold it! Hold it!" To keep your dog from getting into a bad habit, NEVER let her drop an object without scolding her.

60

Cuff her nose lightly, say "Phooey!" then take the object from the floor or the ground (or have the dog reach for it), and make her hold it again. After a few moments, command "Out!" and take the object away.

You may have succeeded in teaching your dog the RETRIEVE ON FLAT exercise in play, but to show real obedience, she must still retrieve on command while the leash is on. When the time comes that your dog will start for the dumbbell on the first command, will pick it up, and will return to sit in front without your having had to use the leash (except for a crooked sit or a sloppy finish), try her in strange surroundings. Do short retrieves at first, then gradually lengthen the distance until the dog, on the first command, will dash out thirty to forty feet to get the dumbbell.

The praise which is given WITH every command while your dog is learning is gradually delayed: (1) To the point at which the dog is picking the dumbbell off the floor; (2) to the time when she has the dumbbell in her mouth and has started back; (3) until after she has come back and is sitting in front; and (4) to the time when she has delivered the dumbbell and has gone to heel position.

Paint your dumbbell white or a bright color. On certain types of floor, or in tall grass, a natural wood dumbbell is hard to see.

Practice THROWING the dumbbell. When you release it, give it a backhanded flip. This will help it land on a wooden floor without rolling or bouncing off to the side.

Finally, make home-retrieving fairly difficult, so that your dog will be dependable when in the Obedience ring.

Things To Remember When Teaching The RETRIEVE ON FLAT

Keep your dog on leash, so you will be ready for that first important correction.

During the early lessons, place the dumbbell directly in front of the dog so that she can reach it by lowering her head.

Give the command ONCE, without body motion.

Follow the command with generous praise. The praise may even encourage your dog to start without a correction.

When a correction is necessary, give extra praise as you jerk the leash.

Give the first command in a happy tone of voice. Save the demanding tone until you need it.

When the leash is off, if your dog fails to start, reach back with your RIGHT foot and tap the dog's right flank while you are saying "Good Girl!" Then rush forward and encourage her to pick up the dumbbell.

Never let your dog come back without the dumbbell. Run forward. Block her! Repeat the command in a more demanding tone, then follow the second command with praise.

When a dog successfully learns to RETRIEVE ON FLAT, the RETRIEVE OVER HURDLE will not be difficult. The wise owner will, however, overcome as many dumbbell problems as he can before requiring his dog to combine retrieving with jumping.

RETRIEVE ON FLAT Problems—How To Overcome Them

Dog Doesn't Start On First Command

See RETRIEVE ON FLAT for ON-leash training.

For off-leash correction, give the command, and if the dog doesn't start, reach back with your RIGHT foot and tap her lightly on the right flank. Give praise as you do so, then rush forward and encourage the dog to pick up the dumbbell.

If your dog is foot-shy because you previously made a bad correction, "spank" the dog forward with your left hand, giving praise!

In extremely stubborn cases, an assistant faces the owner and her dog, and holds the leash at its full length. The dumbbell is placed between them. The owner gives the retrieve command and follows the command with praise. If the dog fails to start, the assistant pulls the dog forward, toward the dumbbell, with one snap of the leash. The owner then runs forward and encourages the dog to pick up the dumbbell.

Dog Anticipates Retrieve

Tell your dog "Stay!" and throw the dumbbell. If the dog starts before you give the command, pivot quickly and WALK AWAY from the dumbbell. As you turn, DEMAND "Heel!" The obedient dog will resist her desire to chase the dumbbell and will remain at heel position. Circle around, return to where you were originally standing, then give the retrieve command.

Alternate correction: After you throw the dumbbell, ask an assistant to pick it up and hand it to you to throw again. Or, pick it up yourself while the dog remains sitting.

RETRIEVE ON FLAT Problems—How To Overcome Them

Dog Is Slow When Going For The Dumbbell

See RETRIEVE ON FLAT for ON-leash training. When you snap the leash, do it forcefully. The dog **knows** the exercise and is merely being lazy.

When the leash is off, there is little you can do except to chase the dog, spank her rear in play, or toss something at her heels, then run forward in a playful manner and encourage her to speed up.

Dog Returns Without The Dumbbell

Hold your leash or some other small object that you can throw. When your dog starts back without the dumbbell, block her by tossing whatever you are holding directly in front of her. Rush forward, pick up the dumbbell, toss it at her feet, and repeat the command in a more demanding tone.

Dog Is Slow To Return After Retrieve

After your dog picks up the dumbbell, turn and RUN, or turn your back and clap your hands. The dog may instinctively speed up. If not, ask an assistant to stand where she will not be seen. Just as the dog slows to a walk, the assistant tosses something in back of her, then ducks out of sight. Four things are important: (1) Do not let the dog see the object when it is thrown; (2) give praise WITH the correction; (3) have the object thrown ONLY when necessary; (4) clap your hands in a playful manner after the correction.

Dog Stands Over Dumbbell Without Picking It Up, Or Stands Holding It

See RETRIEVE ON FLAT for ON-leash training.

Off-leash correction: WHEN THE DOG ISN'T LOOKING, toss some object at her feet, to take her by surprise. Run forward, repeat the command, then run backward, giving praise in a cajoling voice to encourage her to return with the dumbbell.

An assistant can make the correction by tossing the object from a hiding place, providing the dog doesn't see her do it. Having an assistant make the correction is especially effective when the dog just stands and glares at the owner.

RETRIEVE ON FLAT Problems—How To Overcome Them

Dog Refuses To Release Dumbbell

Hold one end of the dumbbell and command "Out!" Wait a moment, then cuff the dog's nose ONCE with the free hand. Say "Good Girl!" after she lets go.

Dog Grabs Dumbbell From The Owner's Hand

Carry the dumbbell in your left hand, and a small, rolled magazine in your right. When the dog grabs for the dumbbell, flip the magazine in front of your body and cuff her on the nose. After the correction, stroke her head with the dumbbell. If she grabs for it again, repeat the correction.

Dog Grabs The Dumbbell When Steward Or Judge Hands It To The Owner

Ask an assistant to hold the dumbbell in one hand, and a rolled magazine in the other, keeping both together. When the dog grabs for the dumbbell, the assistant flips the rolled magazine at the dog's nose, then backs away. Repeat this correction until the dog will quietly accept the dumbbell WITHOUT grabbing.

Dog Mouths Dumbbell

You may never completely overcome your dog's mouthing but if you follow these suggestions, she may mouth her dumbbell less:

(1) Use a dumbbell made of hard wood, such as maple. The harder the material, the better.

(2) Select a dumbbell with the centerpiece no wider than the dog's mouth.

(3) Discourage jaw movement by cuffing the dog under the chin whenever she moves the dumbbell in her mouth, and telling her "Stop that!"

(4) Train your dog to carry things that are breakable, such as raw eggs, or a small balloon. If what the dog is carrying breaks as the result of her playing with it, she may learn to carry with gentleness.

(5) When your dog is at a distance and starts rolling the dumbbell around on her teeth, warn her with "Easy! Easy!"

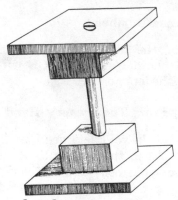

One way to teach your dog the proper way to pick up the dumbbell

Dog Picks Up Dumbbell By The End Instead Of Centerpiece

On each end of the dumbbell, fasten a square block of wood large enough that the dog can't get her mouth around it. Tell her "Stay!" and PLACE the dumbbell some distance away. Return to your dog, tell her "Take it!" and let the dog figure out how to take the dumbbell from the floor. When she learns to use the centerpiece, gradually reduce the size of the end pieces, until you can remove them altogether.

Dog Drops Dumbbell At Handler's Feet

After your dog returns with the dumbbell, and just before she sits in front, do an about-turn and command "Heel!" Come to a halt, then command "Sit! Stay!" "Good Girl!" Practice this until your dog will hold the dumbbell while sitting at heel position. Later, when she brings the dumbbell to you and sits in front, use the "Stay!" command, followed by "Good Girl!" Eventually she won't need the voice command.

Dog Anticipates Finish After Retrieve

Take the dumbbell while your dog is sitting in front. Wait a moment, then pivot back to heel position on your LEFT foot. If the dog moves before you give her permission, DEMAND "Stay!"

In practice, take the dumbbell, then stand up straight, wait a moment, and give the dumbbell back to the dog. Straighten up, wait, then take the dumbbell a second time. If the dog starts to heel position without permission, tell her emphatically "STAY!"

RETRIEVE OVER HIGH JUMP

Before teaching the RETRIEVE OVER HIGH JUMP exercise, train your dog in the jumping part WITHOUT the dumbbell. Never correct for such things as not jumping, or for poor sits and finishes, while your dog is learning the retrieve part of the exercise.

Take your position in front of a low Solid Hurdle with your dog at your left side. Hold the leash in BOTH hands, as when teaching the heeling exercises. As you step toward the jump, command "Robin, Hup!" and snap the leash over the hurdle AHEAD of the dog. Slacken the leash while the dog is jumping, so you won't throw her off balance when she lands. Command "Come!" and jerk the leash toward you, with praise, to make her jump back. Run backward at the same time, gathering up the leash, so the dog will have room to sit squarely in front. If she isn't sitting straight, correct her, then stand erect. Wait a moment, then lean over and pat her. Patting your dog at this point accustoms her to the body movement she will experience when you lean over to take the dumbbell, which you will do in the regular RETRIEVE OVER HIGH JUMP exercise. Stand up a second time, then command the "finish."

When your dog will jump the hurdle both going and coming, and will sit squarely in front on the return, without corrections, do the exercise while the dog holds the dumbbell. Remember to straighten all crooked sits; and after you take the dumbbell, give it back once or twice to keep the dog from anticipating the finish.

Next comes the period of chasing the dumbbell over the hurdle in play—that is, if your dog can be baited with play. Keep the dog on leash. Get her excited. In a teasing way, toss the dumbbell over a LOW hurdle and see if she will go for it. Give ONE command, and, while she is picking up the dumbbell, give lots of praise. Encourage her to jump back, and use the command "Sit! Stay!" to help her keep the dumbbell in her mouth. After she is sitting straight, pat her, take the dumbbell, and complete the exercise.

After your dog plays this game for awhile, tell her "Stay!" and throw the dumbbell. Wait this time for it to stop rolling, then see if she will start when you give the command. Play combined with obedience in this exercise gets excellent results when you have a dog with a frisky nature. Unfortunately, too many dogs have never learned how to play. For them it is straight obedience.

The next step in teaching RETRIEVE OVER HIGH JUMP is to see that the dog not only waits for you to tell her to get the dumbbell, but also that she starts on the first command. Keep the jump LOW, and have the dog on leash. Assume your position close to the hurdle SO YOU WON'T HAVE TO MOVE YOUR FEET when you make a correction. Tell your dog "Stay!" and place the dumbbell on the opposite side of the jump, close enough that you can reach it by leaning over the hurdle. Hold the leash in both hands, and, WITHOUT MOVING YOUR ARMS, say a quiet "Take it!" "Good Girl!" If she starts, fine! That is what you want. If she remains sitting, correct as you did in the RETRIEVE ON FLAT exercise. Jerk the leash ONCE toward the jump while you are saying "Good Girl!" and after the dog jumps, lean over the hurdle, point to the dumbbell, and encourage her to pick it up.

Dogs frequently leap the hurdle when given the retrieve command, but will start back without the dumbbell. In this case, block the dog so she can't return. Cuff her nose gently with the BACK OF YOUR HAND, then jerk her collar toward the dumbbell, using a more demanding "TAKE THAT!"

When your dog will retrieve successfully over a low hurdle on leash, try it without. If she jumps and picks up the dumbbell, rush forward, pat the top board of the hurdle to encourage her to jump back, then back up quickly, giving her room to land. Straighten all crooked sits, take the dumbbell, wait to see if she anticipates the finish, then let her go to heel position on command.

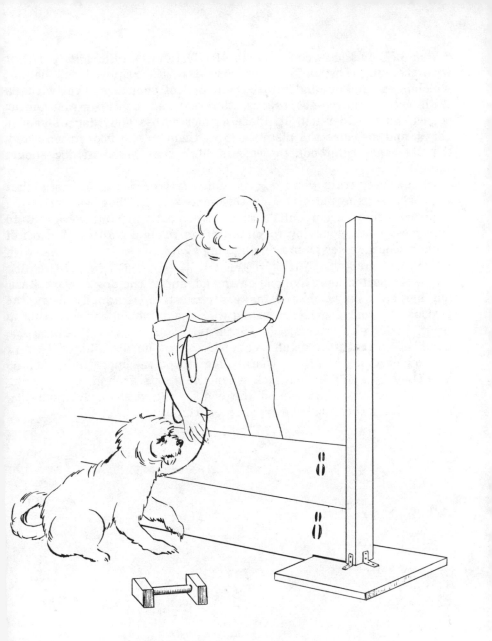

If a dog starts back without the dumb-
bell, block her! Use the back of your hand.

Your dog must be reliable in the RETRIEVE OVER HIGH JUMP with the jump low, before you raise it to the required full height, which is one and one-half times the height of your dog at the withers. With certain heavy-set breeds, the required height measurement equals the shoulder height. Place a ruler across your dog's shoulder bones, and measure the distance from them to the floor; then study the Obedience rule book to see how high your breed of dog should jump.

In practice, train your dog to jump two or three inches higher than will be expected of her in Obedience Trials. This will make the required height seem child's play in comparison; but never go to extremes or ask your dog to jump unreasonable distances. A bad fall could discourage her from ever jumping again.

As you progress in the RETRIEVE OVER HIGH JUMP EXERCISE, strive for perfection. Give one command, and if the dog doesn't start, put her back on leash and make a correction. Gradually delay the praise until your dog has returned with the dumbbell and is sitting in front. Straighten crooked sits. Even test your dog by throwing the dumbbell so that it lands off to one side of the hurdle. This will tempt her to go around, and if she does, will give you the opportunity to stop her. Only by being called back when she starts around, or by being blocked from running around the end on the return, will your dog learn to jump the hurdle both going and coming.

Things To Remember When Teaching RETRIEVE OVER HIGH JUMP

Train your dog to jump and retrieve in play, but keep the dog on leash.

Keep the jump low for the first serious lessons.

Stand close to the hurdle so you can place (or throw) the dumb-bell where you can reach it by leaning over the hurdle.

Give ONE command.

Follow the command with PRAISE.

If the dog fails to start, jerk the leash ONCE while you are giving the praise.

If the dog starts without a correction, give praise just the same.

If your dog leaps the hurdle, then starts back without the dumb-bell, BLOCK her! Cuff her nose with the back of your hand, lean over the hurdle, jerk the leash once toward the dumbbell, and give a more demanding "TAKE THAT!"

Attempts to go around the hurdle on the way out can be stopped by giving the leash a backward snap.

Attempts to come around on the way back, when the leash is off, can be stopped by tossing something in front of the dog to block her. This correction should be made as the dog is passing the hurdle. If given too early, the dog will hesitate about coming back at all.

Practice throwing the dumbbell off to one side, so your dog will have to go out of her way to leap the hurdle on the return.

Practice in strange surroundings, and give the dog only a single chance. Afterward, change the location of the jump.

Dog Starts Toward The Hurdle, Then Stops And Refuses To Jump

Before you correct a dog for refusing to jump, be sure that she is capable of jumping: When a dog gives the impression of wanting to jump by teetering back and forth, but lacks the courage, suspect some form of hip trouble painful to her. Consult your veterinarian, and if necessary, request that the dog's hips be X-rayed.

If refusing the jump is a matter of being obstinate, see RETRIEVE OVER HIGH JUMP for ON-leash training. If the leash is off, rush forward, and with your LEFT hand, "spank" the dog on the rump when she stops. Give praise as you do it.

Dog Returns Without The Dumbbell

When your dog starts back without the dumbbell, rush forward! Block her! Lean over the hurdle, cuff her nose ONCE with the back of your hand, then step over or walk around the hurdle and, if necessary, pick up the dumbbell and toss it at her feet with a more demanding "TAKE THAT!" When she picks it up, pat the top board and coax her to jump back.

Dog Picks Up The Dumbbell But Doesn't Jump Back

Place the hurdle in such a way that an assistant can hide in back of the place where the dumbbell will land. If the dog stops at the jump on the way back, waiting for a second command, the assistant lightly tosses a rolled magazine (or similar object) at the dog's heels. The owner covers up the correction by clapping her hands in play, giving exaggerated praise to encourage the dog after the correction.

Dog Appears Afraid Of The Retrieve Command

Change commands! If you have been using "Take it!" for the retrieve, give the jumping command instead. Combine words, such as "Hup! Take it! Come!" then gradually eliminate commands until you find one of which the dog is no longer afraid.

The assistant's position for the dog that won't start on command.

Dog Doesn't Start On First Command

See RETRIEVE ON FLAT Problems.

In extremely stubborn cases, an assistant stands on the opposite side of a low hurdle and holds the leash at its full length. The owner gives the retrieve command, following the command WITH PRAISE. If the dog fails to start, the assistant pulls the dog forward toward the jump, with one snap of the leash. The owner runs forward, encouraging the dog to jump and to pick up the dumbbell.

Time all corrections!

Dog Goes Around Hurdle Going Out

An assistant stands on the opposite side of the hurdle, quite some distance away, and faces the owner and her dog. If the dog attempts to go around either end, the assistant waits until the dog is on line with the hurdle, then tosses some object (a flat board is excellent) to block her. The owner recalls the dog, then rushes forward, pats the top of the hurdle, encouraging the dog to jump.

RETRIEVE OVER HIGH JUMP Problems—How to Overcome Them

Dog Goes Around Hurdle On The Return

Make a correction first, on leash. Have your dog jump the hurdle; just as she lands, call out a loud "COME!" Follow by snapping the leash toward you to make the dog jump back. Do not make the dog retrieve the dumbbell during the correction.

For off-leash correction, the owner holds some object she can easily throw. When the dog starts to go around the jump on the return, and again when the dog's head is in line with the hurdle, the owner blocks the dog by tossing whatever she is holding directly in front of the dog. After this, she rushes forward, pats the top board, and encourages the dog to come over the top.

NOTE: When correcting a dog for running around the hurdle, it is important that the correction be made at the right time. If the object is thrown too soon, the owner PREVENTS a mistake, instead of correcting it. The dog may also be frightened, and will hesitate to come back at all.

Dog Doesn't Clear The Hurdle

If there is no indication of hip dysplasia, or the dog is not over-weight, ask two assistants to stand one on each side of the hurdle. One assistant holds a light rod (bamboo or aluminum) so that it rests along the top board, slightly lower than the board itself. The second assistant is there merely to keep the dog from going around the opposite end. With the dog on leash, teach her first to clear the hurdle without retrieving. Give the jumping command, and while the dog is jumping, have the assistant raise the rod and rap her paws lightly. The severity with which the correction is made depends upon the size of the dog and on her temperament. Give praise WITH all corrections.

An alternate method is for the assistant to move a short rod from one side of the jump to the other, parallel to the floor, while the dog is jumping. This EXTENDS the jump, which raises it.

See RETRIEVE ON FLAT problems for corrections of the following: Dog Anticipates Retrieve—Dog Stands Over Dumbbell, Or Stands Holding Dumbbell—Dog Refuses To Release Dumbbell—Dog Grabs At Dumbbell In The Owner's Hand—Dog Grabs The Dumbbell From Steward Or Judge—Dog Anticipates Finish—Dog Drops Dumbbell At Handler's Feet—Dog Mouths Dumbbell—Dog Picks Up Dumbbell By The End Instead Of The Centerpiece.

THE BROAD JUMP

It is assumed that your dog is familiar with the BROAD JUMP, having learned to leap the individual hurdles in play, as described in the JUMPING exercise. To prepare your dog for the BROAD JUMP as it is done in Obedience Trials, place the individual hurdles close together and tip them on their sides. This will take away temptation, teaching your dog to clear the hurdles from the very beginning.

Put your dog on leash and leave her on a sit-stay in front of the first hurdle. Take your position to the right of the jump, with your left shoulder turned slightly away from the dog. Hold the handle of the leash in your right hand, and support the weight of the leash in your left, held at arm's length, directly above the center of the jump. WITHOUT MOVING YOUR ARMS, give the jumping command, which may be "Hup!" "Jump!" or "Over!" Follow the command with "Good Girl!" and snap the leash **forward.** While the dog is landing, command "Come! Good Girl!" snap the leash toward you, then coax her to come close and sit squarely in front. So she can do a proper finish, make a quarter turn to the right while the dog is jumping. After she is sitting in front, pat her, then complete the exercise by having her go to heel position. If your dog will start on the jumping command, don't jerk the leash, but give praise just the same. The two things to remember when teaching the BROAD JUMP are: (1) Give the command without moving your arms; and (2) give

Give the jumping command WITHOUT arm motion.

praise while the dog is jumping, whether you jerk the leash or not.

The show ring procedure for the BROAD JUMP requires the handler to stand two feet away from the jump, facing it, and within the area of the first and last hurdles. While the dog is jumping, the handler is permitted to make a forty-five-degree angle turn to the right, to enable the dog to sit squarely in front and do a proper finish. To accustom your dog to the BROAD JUMP as it is done in Obedience Trials, follow this procedure in practice as you increase the over-all length by stages with the hurdles upright, in their proper position. The required BROAD JUMP length is twice that which your dog jumps in height.

During practice, set up the BROAD JUMP in a new location. Give the dog a single chance, then move the jump again. Make her leap the jump in reverse direction, jumping from the high point to the low. Turn the individual hurdles on their backs to give the jump an unusual appearance. This prepares a dog for unexpected situations at Obedience Trials, where conditions are not always ideal.

Things To Remember When Teaching The BROAD JUMP

Keep the dog on leash until she knows how to jump.

Keep the jump narrow while making leash corrections.

Stand with your back slightly toward the dog.

Hold the leash in BOTH hands.

Give the command WITHOUT MOVING YOUR ARMS.

If the dog doesn't start, or if she attempts to amble across, jerk the leash FORWARD while you are giving the praise.

Snap the leash parallel to the ground.

Slacken the leash while the dog is landing.

At the moment of landing, call out a forceful "Come!" and snap the leash toward you, giving extra praise.

Practice in strange surroundings.

Practice with BROAD JUMPS unusual in appearance.

BROAD JUMP Problems—How To Overcome Them

Dog Anticipates Jumping Command

Alternate the Sit-stay with the Jumping command. Leave your dog sitting in front of the first hurdle. Take your position to the right of the jump. Wait a few moments, then return to heel position. Leave your dog again. Do this until the dog no longer anticipates the Jumping command. If she starts before she is told, tell her emphatically, "STAY!"

Dog Doesn't Jump On First Command Or Signal

See page 40 for on-leash training.

Off-leash correction: Ask an assistant to stand close to and directly in back of your dog. Give the Jumping command and follow the command with praise. If the dog doesn't start, ask the assistant to tap the dog gently with the toe of her shoe. Your praise and the clapping of your hands should convince the dog the correction was sort of "accidental." An alternate correction is to toss something in back of her when she doesn't start, providing she is not the scary type; but the most satisfactory method of overcoming this BROAD JUMP problem is to teach your dog that "Jump!" means jump, best accomplished through proper timing when the leash is on.

One way to teach your dog to jump higher.

Dog Doesn't Jump High Enough

Put your dog on leash. (The leash is to keep the dog from running around the ends.) Ask two assistants to stand, one on each side of the hurdle, and to hold the bar from the Bar Jump between them, directly above the jump. The height should be equal to what the dog jumps when retrieving over the hurdle. Make the dog jump back and forth several times so she will learn to jump height as well as breadth.

One way to teach your dog not to walk on the jump.

Dog Walks Over Broad Jump

Ask two assistants to stand, one on each side of the hurdle, and to hold the bar of the Bar Jump between them but lower than the top of the first hurdle. With your dog on leash, give the Jumping command. Follow the command with praise. If your dog starts to amble across, ask the assistants to raise the bar and move it parallel to the floor in the direction the dog is jumping. In the meantime, use the leash and pull the dog across. The moving of the bar lengthens the over-all jump and by doing this over and over, your dog may learn to leap the full Broad Jump length.

If there is no one to assist, secure a piece of chicken wire or hardware cloth. Lay this on top of the jump. If, after two or three tries, your dog clears the jump, fool her by working the wire under one hurdle at a time. Later, take it away entirely.

By using ingenuity, you may discover your own cure for the dog that walks on top of the Broad Jump. Design a jump that will "give." One that will trip. Or, place on top something other than chicken wire that your dog will want to avoid.

BROAD JUMP Problems—How To Overcome Them

Dog Goes Wide On The Return

With your dog on leash, and ready for the jump, give the command and the moment she lands on the opposite side, call out a loud "COME!" then snap the leash hard. After you snap it, give praise and coax her to sit close, then pat her. When you take the leash off, use a forceful command.

Dog Walks To Owner Without Jumping

Hold the bar from the Bar Jump, or the two or four inch board from the Solid Hurdle, vertically in your left hand. When the dog starts to amble toward you instead of jumping, drop the bar or the board directly in front of her. After you block her, encourage her to jump by grabbing the collar and helping her across.

An assistant can make the correction by standing a few feet away to the dog's right and holding the bar or the board in her right hand. When the dog cuts toward the owner, the object is made to fall directly in the dog's path. The owner then playfully encourages the dog to jump as she should.

Dog Cuts Corners To The Right

Stand close to the jump. Give the Jumping command and WHILE THE DOG IS LANDING, lift your knee or your foot and bump the dog as she comes down. Pat her!

Dog Cuts Corners To The Left

The same, but have an assistant do the "bumping." Off-leash corrections can be made by having two assistants, one on each side of the jump. If the dog cuts to either side, one of the assistants drops something as if by accident. The noise should make the dog veer toward the center of the jump.

One way to cure cutting corners!

SIT- AND DOWN-STAYS

When training your dog to stay while you go out of sight, leave one way, then return from another direction. The element of surprise, not knowing from which direction you MIGHT return, will help your dog to settle down and wait more contentedly.

Practice the stays as part of your dog's daily routine, and practice in strange places. Staying on command should not be associated entirely with the training yard and the Obedience ring.

Alternate the STAY exercises with the RECALL so your dog will distinguish more clearly between the "STAY!" command and that of "Come!"

SIT- And DOWN-STAY Problems—How To Overcome Them

Dog Creeps On Stays

Fasten a long line to your dog's collar. Ask an assistant to hold the end, out of sight, in back of the dog. (The line can be run through a crack in the door or through shrubbery or bushes.) When the dog inches forward, the line is jerked sharply.

SIT- And DOWN-STAY Problems—How To Overcome Them

Dog Refuses To Stay

Ask an assistant to stand behind your dog and hold the handle of the leash. Whenever she moves, the assistant jerks the dog back to position.

If the dog breaks only occasionally, tempt her so you can get in a good correction. Put your dog on a long line, and ask an assistant to hold the end out of sight in back of the dog. Tell your dog "Stay!" Face her across the training area. Kneel, tap the ground, clap your hands, run, but **don't call your dog.** If the other antics cause the dog to move, call out a forceful "STAY!" before the assistant jerks the line.

Dog Rolls Over On Back When Put Down For The Down-Stay

Put your dog on leash. Command "Down!" and pull down on the leash. When the dog settles to the floor, call out firmly, "STAY!" If she rolls over in spite of the warning, quickly lift her to a sitting position, then again tell her "Down! STAY!" When the dog will lie down properly with the leash on, remove the leash but continue with the verbal command of "STAY!" after the dog goes down, until the extra command is no longer necessary.

Dog Sniffs Other Dogs

Train your dog to stay away from other dogs! Station a dog on either side of yours, and ask two assistants to stand close to them. If your dog runs to either of the others, ask the assistant to cuff your dog's muzzle with the back of her hand, or to flick a small, rolled magazine in your dog's face. Take her back where she was and try again.

SIT- And DOWN-STAY Problems—How To Overcome Them

Dog Sits Up On The Down

An assistant stands close to the dog while she is in the Down position. If the dog lifts herself to a sitting position, the assistant quickly taps her on the nose to make her lie down again. After the correction the assistant scratches the dog's ear or pats her.

Alternate correction: Put the dog on a long line and run it through a ring on the floor or in the ground close to the dog's front paws. While an assistant holds the end, some distance away or out of sight, tempt your dog. Run, play with another dog, slam the door of your car or clap your hands. If your dog can't stand the activities, and gets up, call out "STAY!" and let the assistant pull the dog down by jerking the line.

Dog Lies Down During The SIT And STAY

If your dog lies down when you are at a distance, try sliding something along a slippery floor toward her, or toss something underneath her to make her jump up to a sitting position.

Alternate correction: Use the leash or fasten a thin line to the dog's collar, then hook it to some object above the dog's head, leaving it slack enough that the dog won't feel the pull, yet not so slack as to permit the dog to lie down.

Correct the dog that lies down without permission by sauntering back until you are directly in front of the dog; then QUICKLY reach out with your foot and tap or scuff into her paws. Follow by patting.

Lying down from a Sit, or sitting from the Down, can sometimes be cured by surprising the dog when she changes position. The owner or an assistant watches from a hidden spot, and, when the dog moves, something is dropped close by to startle the dog, making her think her movement was the cause of what happened.

NOTE: This type of correction should not be made in a training class where there are other dogs that are behaving, or they will be confused.

If your dog is not afraid of strangers, ask someone to put your dog in the correct position when she breaks. If the dog thinks the judge or the steward at a dog show will do the same, she may have more respect for YOUR stay command.

One way to overcome the DOWN-STAY problem.

One way to keep your dog from lying down on the SIT-STAY.

SIT- And DOWN-STAY Problems—How To Overcome Them

Correcting the dog that gets up without permission.

Dog Sits When Handler Returns After The Down And Stay

When you return to your dog after the Down-stay, and find her sitting, or if she gets up while you are circling, cuff her sharply on the end of the nose and put her down again. Wait a few moments, then pat her while she is in the Down position.

Dog Whines During Sit- And Down-Stays

The following suggestions may be effective, if not a cure:

1) Train your dog, as much as possible, to stay alone.
2) Use a water gun (have an assistant use one, also) and squirt water at her whenever she whines.
3) Muzzle the dog temporarily with a piece of gauze bandage. When she is quiet, take the bandage off. When she whines, put it on again.
4) Consult your veterinarian. Ask if he recommends a tranquilizer to calm your dog's nerves.

A dog that has learned to stay alone will be less inclined to whine or to break the Stays than the dog that always has companionship. Train your dog to be independent so that she will feel secure when left alone.

GENERAL Problems—How To Overcome Them

Inattentiveness

Correct your dog every time she looks away. Jerk the leash, bump into her, tumble her by catching her off guard. Use any trick you can to make your dog watch you while she is in training. Praise with all corrections and the dog will not resent them.

Sniffing The Ground

Every time your dog lowers her head, jerk up on the leash without saying anything. If she is off leash, throw something or kick at the spot the dog is sniffing.

Dog Follows Handler When Left For Drop On Recall Or Stay Exercises

Carry an object in your LEFT hand. This can be a rolled magazine, or the leash wadded into a ball. When you leave your dog, ask an assistant to watch. If the dog moves, have the assistant call out "Throw it," in which case, toss the object BACKWARD, so it lands at the dog's feet. Take her back and try again.

Alternate correction: When you leave your dog, BACK AWAY. Hold something that you can throw to check the dog when she starts forward. RUN toward her at the same time, and put her back where she was.

Barks While Working

Carry a small, rolled-up magazine! When the dog barks, throw it at the dog's feet, or have an assistant toss the magazine for you. After the correction, give praise and clap your hands in a playful manner.

Dog Does Not Sit Close In Front

Use only your voice and a coaxing motion with your hands. Avoid moving your feet. As your dog slows down, or comes to a sitting position, quietly but firmly repeat, "Come, come, come!" until she moves forward of her own accord. When she does, reward her with a pat or a tasty morsel.

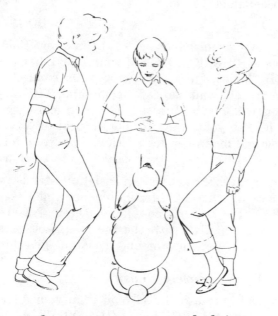

One way to correct crooked sits.

Crooked Sit In Front

Practice with the dog on leash. With the dog facing you, hold the leash in BOTH hands. Walk backward and take the dog with you. Come to a halt, wait for her to Sit at an angle, THEN pull the leash taut and spank whichever hip is out of line. The handler should CORRECT rather than PREVENT crooked Sits. In other words, let the dog start to Sit crooked **before** you make the correction. Hold the leash tight, and give praise as you do it. When the leash is off, hold the collar instead.

Alternate correction: Two assistants stand facing each other, one on either side, and close to the handler. When the dog starts to swing her rear end out of line, an assistant gently taps the dog on the hip, while the handler coaxes the dog to come close and Sit straight. A persistent "Sit straight! Sit straight!" should teach the dog to correct her own crooked Sits.

GENERAL Problems—How To Overcome Them

Dog Ignores Command To Go To Heel

LARGE DOGS	SMALL DOGS
Without moving your hands or feet, command "Heel!" THEN with BOTH hands, jerk the leash to your left and as far back as you can reach. Praise as you do it. Pat your knee to turn the dog and make her face front.	Lean over. Hold the leash in your LEFT hand. Without moving your hand or feet, give the command, THEN jerk the leash, low and close to the ground. Give praise WITH the correction. Pat your left leg to coax the dog to turn around.

In extremely stubborn cases, an assistant stands in back of, and off to one side of, the dog (depending on which way she goes to Heel). AFTER the owner's command, the assistant taps the dog on the hip "accidentally" with the toe of a shoe, so she will move around by herself. Both owner and assistant give praise!

Dog Does Not Do A Complete Finish

Wad the leash into a ball and hold it in your LEFT hand. Give the Heel command WITHOUT MOVING YOUR ARM. Let the dog move around to Heel position, and wait for her to Sit at an angle. THEN jerk the leash backward, giving praise.

Sloppy Finishes

For practice, hold the leash, wadded into a ball, in your left hand. Do a series of:

1) Steps to the right
2) Quarter-turn pivots to the left
3) About-turns
4) Steps to the rear

With each change of direction, command "Heel!" and snap the dog to the correct Heel position with praise.

Dog Circles Wide On The Finish When The Leash Is Off

During practice, give the command to Heel, and at the point the dog goes wide, give a SECOND Heel command, forcefully. Praise.

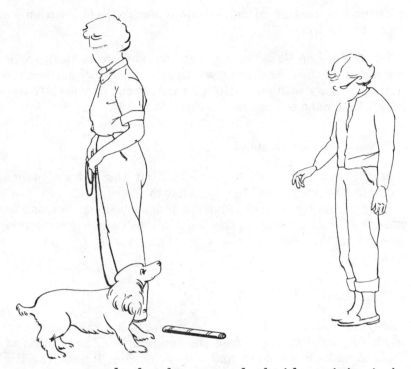

One way to correct the dog that goes to heel without sitting in front.

Dog Goes Directly To Heel Without Sitting In Front

Put your dog on leash. Face her for the Recall. Ask an assistant to stand behind you with a rolled-up magazine. Call your dog. DO NOT use the leash to make her Sit in front. Wait for her to go to Heel without Sitting. THEN have the assistant toss the magazine at your side, directly in front of the dog. After the correction, gather up the leash, make her Sit straight, then praise and pat her. Repeat the exercise but take care the assistant makes the correction ONLY if the dog goes directly to Heel without stopping in front.

The owner can make the correction herself by dropping something at her left side, if the dog is trained to go to the left; or something on the right, if the dog is trained to go to the right.

GENERAL Problems—How To Overcome Them

Dog Turns Out Instead of In, When Going To Heel Position (when going to the left)

Put the dog on leash. Give the command to go to Heel, and if the dog starts to turn the wrong way, spank her hindquarters AWAY from your body with your RIGHT hand; then pat your left leg with your LEFT hand to coax her to turn toward you and Sit close.

Dog Takes Judge's Commands

During practice, have someone call out the judge's commands. Count five before you tell the dog what to do.

If you train by yourself, give the judge's commands aloud before you give the commands to the dog. This will teach your dog not to respond to the sound of the voice, but to wait for definite commands.

Dog Runs Away

If your dog, while heeling, darts away, call her name sharply, reach out and slap her across the rump, or toss something at her heels to make her look around. Pat your side! Repeat the Heeling command, using a more demanding tone and follow the command with praise.

If the dog ignores your commands and runs playfully about, throw a rolled-up magazine, your shoe, the leash, anything, at her heels when she is NOT LOOKING, then drop to a kneeling position, and call her to come to you for protection.

Teaching a dog to come when she is called is a family affair. At home and in the training class, cooperate by making a dog go to whoever calls her. Point to the person who called, and tell the dog "GO!" Even chase her, if necessary!

Station several assistants around the training area, armed with empty cartons. When your dog starts running around and ignores your command to "Come!" ask those who are assisting to block her by tossing the cartons directly in front of her. Kneel, call her again, and give constant praise.

GENERAL Problems—How To Overcome Them

Dog Anticipates Commands

Avoid following a set routine. For instance, alternate the Come with the Sit-stay. If your dog anticipates the "Finish," pivot back to Heel position on your LEFT foot, and don't let her complete the exercise. Throw the dumbbell, but don't let the dog go for it. Place her in front of the Broad Jump, take your position but don't let her jump. Any time she moves WITHOUT permission, DEMAND "Stay!" emphatically.

School's out!

SUGGESTIONS FOR THOSE WHO EXHIBIT IN
OPEN OBEDIENCE CLASSES

Give your dog sufficient training, so you will feel confident when you enter the Obedience ring.

Read the Obedience rule book carefully! Familiarize yourself with show ring procedure. The extra commands, signals, and body gestures you used to train your dog are not permitted in a regular trial. Careless handling can cause your dog to fail.

Train your dog in unfamiliar surroundings to prepare for the unexpected. Conditions at dog shows are not always ideal.

When you enter the show grounds, keep your dog from sniffing. If she lowers her head, jerk up on the leash to make her pay attention. Sniffing is a major problem of Obedience exhibitors.

The majority of dogs are at their best when they have been left alone prior to competing. Staying by herself even for only a few moments may alert your dog and make her anxious to please.

Exercise your dog and give her a drink of water before your turn comes to enter the ring. If the dog is to do her best work, she must be as comfortable as possible. Groom her for appearances' sake.

Take time to observe the class routine for that day. Judges usually follow the same pattern for each exhibitor. Should you fail to hear a command while your dog is working, you will have some idea of what to expect.

When in the Obedience ring, walk briskly and move in a straight line. Keep your corners square, and when you do an about-turn, pivot smoothly without fancy footwork. Some handlers take a step backward before they turn, which leaves the dog behind.

When the judge calls for a "Fast!" change to a running pace instead of just walking faster. In the "Slow!" avoid sauntering or your dog will want to sit down. When it is time for "The Figure 8" take your position facing the judge. In doing "The Figure 8," you can go in whichever direction you please. Walk naturally, and let your dog change pace.

For the "drop," **you** be the judge of whether to use voice or a hand signal. If your dog faces a brightly lighted window, and would therefore have trouble seeing your raised arm, use a verbal command. When there is noise, and lots of distractions, give the command with more than usual authority. If you prefer the signal, train your dog to drop while your fingers are pointing up. A motion toward the floor could be interpreted as the signal to come; but more important, some judges consider an up-and-down motion a double signal and would fail your dog, or give her a penalty.

For the RETRIEVE ON FLAT, keep your voice happy. Your dog may not be reliable on the Retrieve exercise, but she **might** respond this time because of **your** cheerful attitude.

When you come to the RETRIEVE OVER HIGH JUMP decide whether to use the Retrieve or the Jumping command. The "Take it!" will sometimes cause a dog to run around a hurdle, but the "Jump!" or "Hup!" may make her go over, and when she sees the dumbbell on the other side, she will automatically pick it up.

For both the RETRIEVE ON FLAT and the RETRIEVE OVER HIGH JUMP, use a light-colored dumbbell; and when you throw it, give a backhand twist to your wrist. This will keep the dumbbell from rolling. The fact that the dumbbell is light-colored will make it easy for your dog to see.

For the DROP ON RECALL and the Retrieve exercises, stand away from the side of the ring, or from objects in the ring. If there is little space in back of you, your dog may hesitate to go completely around. Give her room to do a good finish.

The BROAD JUMP requires a forceful command with emphasis on the "Hup!" or "JUMP!"—not on the dog's name. Teach your dog a definite Jump command and she will be more reliable when doing the BROAD JUMP in strange surroundings.

During the SIT- and DOWN-STAY exercises, place your armband and leash far enough away that your dog won't be tempted to sniff them. If it is the LONG SIT, have your dog Sitting squarely on both hips. If it is the LONG DOWN, leave her resting comfortably on one hip. Give the Stay command and signal together, but don't use your dog's name. **Avoid yelling** and when you leave, step out on your right foot from an upright position. Crouching encourages a dog to follow.

In practice, train your dog to lie down at Heel position when you give a signal with your left hand. The left hand held close to the floor, with wrist bent, is the signal for lying down at Heel position. The dog must go down on signal or command. She cannot be put down with the hand on the collar or the dog.

After your dog's performance, if you are pleased with the way she worked, don't be ashamed to show it. If you aren't pleased, let the spectators think you are anyway! Avoid harsh corrections, or publicly shaming your dog. Obedience is a sporting game, not to be taken too seriously.

But tell me again, how do I make WILLIE take the dumbbell?

BOOK THREE

UTILITY
OBEDIENCE COURSE
(with Tracking)

CONTENTS for BOOK THREE
UTILITY OBEDIENCE COURSE
(and TRACKING)

The publisher wishes to express thanks to Miss Elinor E. Mason, friend and associate of Miss Saunders, for her assistance in seeing that this new edition is in accord with current Obedience Regulations.

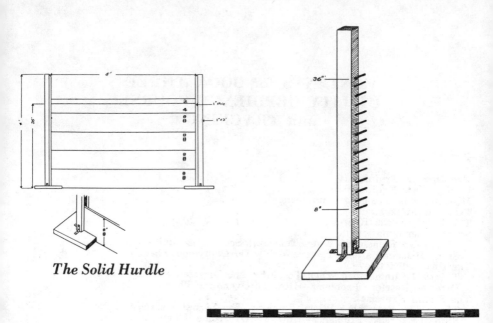

The Solid Hurdle

The Bar Jump

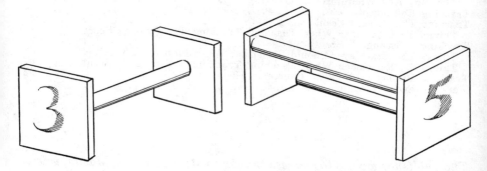

Two popular styles of Scent Discrimination articles. They don't roll! They are easy to pick up.

4

UTILITY CLASS EQUIPMENT

Scent Articles: Two sets, each comprised of five identical articles not more than six inches in length, one set being metal and the other leather. The articles in a set should be legibly numbered one to five.

Directed Retrieve Articles: Three short, predominantly white, work gloves.

The High Jump: Five feet wide. Adjustable in heights of from eight to thirty-six inches. Consists of four 1" x 8" boards, one 1" x 4" board, one 1" x 2" board, and two 4-foot Standard uprights, each with a wide base, constructed with grooves into which the boards fit. (See **Regulations and Standards for Obedience Trials,** available from: The American Kennel Club, 51 Madison Avenue, New York, N.Y. 10010, and The Canadian Kennel Club, 667 Yonge Street, Toronto, Canada.)

The Bar Jump: Construction is similar to that of the High Jump. Instead of boards, a square wooden horizontal bar (2" to 2½" square) is used, which is adjustable for raising or lowering according to the height of the dog. Adjustable for each two inches from 8 up to 36 inches. (See **Regulations and Standards for Obedience Trials**).

A convenient type stake for the line and pulley when practicing the GO in open fields.

MISCELLANEOUS TRAINING EQUIPMENT

Miscellaneous Scent Articles: Small stones, short pieces of pipe, hand tools or other unusual items.

Clip-Board: A piece of ¾" plywood, two to three feet square, equipped with eight clip-type broom holders, or a piece of masonite with holes already drilled.

Long Line: 100 feet of thin plastic or nylon clothesline.

Pulley: Preferably the covered type so the line can't slip off and get jammed around the wheel.

Screw-type Metal Stake: One approximately a foot and a half long, with a swivel ring on the side. (Available at most hardware stores.)

Rolled Magazine: A small, rolled magazine fastened with elastic bands or taped.

For Tracking Equipment, see page 74.

6

TRAINING SUGGESTIONS

Disguise corrections! Don't let your dog blame you or your assistant for unpleasantness.

If you inadvertently make a harsh correction or misjudge the timing, make up to your dog immediately. Take care not to repeat the same mistake.

When you find that one of the suggested corrective methods has a bad effect on **your** dog, don't use it. Dogs react differently to corrections.

When problems come up, work backward. For instance, if your dog consistently takes the wrong scent article, pick up the unscented articles and start from the beginning. If your dog doesn't respond to signals, put the leash on and give her basic training. Praise and a fresh start have a magical effect when a dog is temporarily confused.

When you use your hand to reprimand your dog, such as cuffing her nose for creeping on the STAND, pat her with the SAME hand you used to correct her. Make her think the hand correction was accidental.

During the heeling exercises, if your dog is a slow performer, make leash corrections when she doesn't expect them. The element of surprise keeps a dog alert and makes her responsive.

While attempting to overcome one problem, if your dog slips back in some other part of the exercise, this is to be expected. The setback, while discouraging, is temporary. In time you will balance the training.

Give praise WITH every command and WITH every signal. Give extra praise when you use the leash. This bridges the gap between the giving of a command or signal to your dog and OBEDIENCE, done willingly and with spirit.

Note: The suggestions offered in **The Complete UTILITY Obedience Course** will be more effective if your dog received the training outlined in **The Complete Novice Obedience Course** and **The Complete Open Obedience Course.**

The instructions given in the succeeding sections of this book are for people who are right-handed. Those who are left-handed may follow the same instructions, simply substituting the left hand for the right and the right hand for the left. However, in Obedience Trials, a dog must work on the handler's left side.

THE UTILITY CLASS EXERCISE

Training dogs for the UTILITY Class is comparatively easy when owners PREPARE their dogs for this more advanced work. If your dog is still a puppy, teach her now to carry and retrieve assorted objects. The SCENT DISCRIMINATION exercise is nothing more then retrieving articles with a special scent. Put the articles in unusual places. Use the proper signals throughout the Novice and Open training, and the SIGNAL EXERCISE will be a cinch. The GROUP EXAMINATION, which is only a longer Stand for Examination with the handlers further away, should be fairly easy since your dog has come this far in her training.

This leaves the DIRECTED JUMPING and the DIRECTED Re-TRIEVE as the NEW exercises in the UTILITY Course. Even these can be simplified if, before you throw your dog a glove to catch, you encourage her to "GO!" or if you will stand at the side of the Bar or the Solid Jump, then signal the dog to jump, so she will learn to detour in order to leap the hurdles.

Training for the UTILITY Class, like that for the OPEN Class has greater advantage when approached as a series of exercises. Dogs are at different stages of training during ALL advanced work and while group training can and is being done, it is more practical to deal with UTILITY problems individually. For this reason, the five UTILITY Course exercises and TRACKING will be reviewed separately, first from the teaching angle, and then by listing suggested methods for overcoming problems.

SCENT DISCRIMINATION

SCENT DISCRIMINATION is one of many Obedience exercises that can be started in the house on a rainy day or during a free evening. First, though, your dog must know how to retrieve on command. Select three or four articles made of wood, leather, and metal that your dog enjoys working with, and let her retrieve them, one at a time, in play. When she brings them to you willingly, and with spirit, ask an assistant to scatter a few "odds and ends" around the room, that your dog might be curious about, but would have little desire to pick up. These can be such things as small pieces of heavy iron, tin cans, small cardboard boxes, or even a large stone or two. Don't group the objects closely together and if you place the articles yourself, handle them with a pair of ice or kitchen tongs, available at most hardware stores.

With your dog sitting at heel position and facing the objects, let her retrieve the scent articles she has been working with, from among the strange objects scattered over the floor. Treat this as a RETRIEVE ON FLAT exercise, letting the dog SEE you throw each article. Out of curiosity, your dog will undoubtedly sniff the strange objects and when she does, don't say anything. Let her satisfy her inquisitive nature, and when she goes for her favorite article, the one she has been working with, clap your hands and give praise while she is picking it up.

When your dog is successful in this part of the scent work, cover her eyes as you throw the article. This way she will HEAR, but not see, it drop. Now she will have to use her nose. Remember not to say anything when she sniffs the unscented articles, but the moment her nose touches the scented one, give enthusiastic praise.

Later, leave your dog on a Sit-stay while you **walk** to the group of strange objects and place the scent article you want the dog to bring back. Finally, turn your dog and, **while she is facing away from the objects,** place your article, or have someone do it for you. Cup your hand over the dog's nose and tell her "Find!", and let her go for the article without again sitting at heel. When someone helps with this exercise it doesn't matter if the assistant touches the "odds and ends," but when working alone, the owner must not forget to use tongs when handling the unscented articles.

As your dog becomes dependable in her scent work, change the strange objects from time to time, selecting unscented articles that are similar to the ones you are using, but not identical. Your dog should do nose work of a simple nature and be familiar with the SCENT DISCRIMINATION routine used in Obedience Trials before you tempt her to make mistakes by using articles that look alike.

Slowly and gradually group the unscented articles closer together, and when your dog is ready for the crucial test, replace the "odds and ends," one at a time, with the regular scent discrimination articles. Start with those your dog favors the least so she won't be tempted to pick up the wrong one. When teaching, it is better to prevent mistakes than to make the test difficult and correct the dog too often.

When your dog will select HER two articles from among, let's say, the metal ones, start adding, one at a time, the unscented leather ones, leaving the dog's favorites again until last. Of course, if your dog prefers to work with metal, use the metal for the final test.

Some dogs, at first, simply will not use their nose, but will grab the first article they see. Rather than yell at your dog and frighten her, or scold her for picking up the wrong article, use a clip-board. This can be a piece of ¾-inch plywood, two feet square or larger, equipped with twelve clip-type broom holders into which the unscented articles are fastened, or a piece of masonite with holes already drilled. If you prefer, you may glue the articles to the board itself, or tie them down with a piece of string, or use a peg-board and fasten the articles with rubber bands.

on it. Let your dog see you throw the article, so she won't hesitate to go near this strange-looking object, then, after she retrieves several times and is no longer cautious about the board, toss the article so it lands ON the board, between the unscented articles. Later, cover your dog's eyes so she will have to use her nose to find the right one. If she gets discouraged when she can't find the correct article immediately, the fact that the unscented articles CAN'T be picked up will encourage her to keep hunting. While working, reassure her with "Keep looking! Keep looking!" and when she spots the right article, give praise immediately.

A dog soon gets wise to the fact that the scented article is the one that is NOT in the broom holder, so your next step is to place the scented article ON TOP of an empty broom clip. This way your article will LOOK like the others but it won't be fastened to the board. To make it even more difficult, each time you place your article, change the location on the board. When it is obvious that your dog is using her nose, gradually take the unscented articles out of the holders and scatter THEM over the floor or on the ground around the board. Finally, take away the board and follow the procedure for teaching SCENT DISCRIMINATION.

Whenever your dog picks up the wrong article (and she will), don't yell! If you yell at your dog when she is learning the scent work, she will be afraid to go near the articles, or will hesitate about picking one up in case it is the wrong article. Instead, quietly walk to her, take her by the collar, pry open her mouth to make her drop the article, then shame her in a low voice with "NO!" or "Phooey!" Pick up the right article, toss it at her feet, and tell her, more demandingly, "Take that!"

Another method of training for SCENT DISCRIMINATION is to work entirely on leash; but, here again, your dog must know how to retrieve on command. Stand close to the articles so your dog can reach them without your having to move your feet. Hold the leash lightly in BOTH hands. Place your article, and if the dog starts to pick up the wrong one, DRAG her slowly away, or snap her head up quickly. Don't say anything unless it is a quiet "No!" Then encourage her to keep trying until she finds the right article. When she does, give immediate praise.

When your dog will pick up both articles on the first command while on leash, try it with the leash off, but stand to close the articles. Your dog must work perfectly while you stand at a distance equal to the length of the leash before you put her to the final test where she must work with the articles placed fifteen to twenty feet away.

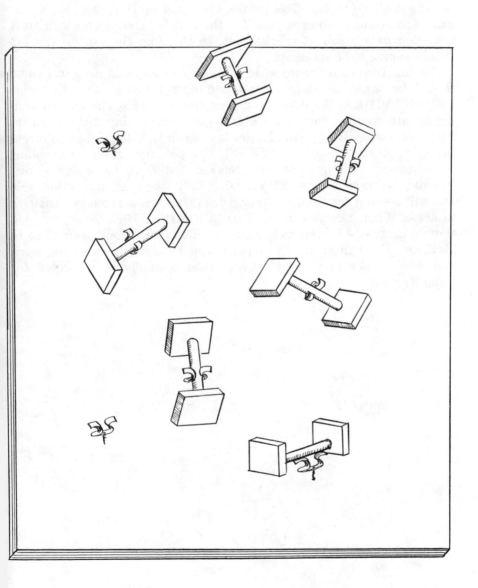

The Clip-board. Simple to make. Easy to transport.

When working without the leash, if your dog fails to START for her scent articles on command, reach back with your RIGHT foot and tap the dog's right hip. Give praise when you do this, then RUN forward and encourage her to look for the article. The kickback to start your dog gets excellent results, but, to the dog, the tap on the hip should appear to be accidental.

Certain factors influence a dog's ability to do good nose work and should be taken into consideration during training. One factor is TEMPERATURE. Scent is more pronounced during the early morning or late evening than at noon on a hot summer day. SUN is an influencing factor, scent being longer lasting in the shade than in direct sunlight. Another factor is ODORS. The potency of tar or gasoline, for instance, when overpowering, makes it difficult for a dog to distinguish between scents. ENVIRONMENT plays an important role and will account for failures among dogs that are nervous or sensitive to noise. When teaching SCENT DISCRIMINATION, give your dog time to acclimate herself to her surroundings with conditions close to ideal and she will probably surprise you by doing good scent work even though she may be of a breed that normally is not noted for using its nose.

Things To Remember When Teaching SCENT DISCRIMINATION

For the preliminary lessons, use your dog's favorite articles and place them among strange looking objects.

Don't yell at your dog when she sniffs a wrong article.

Give praise when the dog sniffs the correct one.

Don't talk while your dog is working. Talking distracts your dog.

Don't place the scented article too close to the unscented ones. Overlapping scent can cause a dog unintentionally to pick up the wrong article.

The praise you give when your dog sniffs the correct article is later delayed until the dog has the article in her mouth. Delay it even further, until your dog has returned and is sitting in front. Finally, withhold it until the exercise has been completed.

If your dog becomes confused in her scent work and grabs just any article, pick up all the articles and start from the beginning. If necessary, use the clip-board for a refresher course.

Correct for picking up the wrong article by walking slowly to your dog. Pry open her mouth so she will drop the article, then jerk the collar toward the right article and encourage her to pick it up.

After your dog **knows** SCENT DISCRIMINATION, change the numbered articles **each time you work.** If the same practice set is used every day, when your dog can't find them during the actual test at an Obedience Trial, she may come back without any.

Use articles your dog can see, especially when working out-of-doors. Failures occur in Obedience Trials when the articles, which the dog didn't see placed, have been hidden by the long grass.

Don't wash your scent articles unless you do so to remove dirt. Air them instead!

Dog Doesn't Start On First Command

This is **retrieve** trouble, not scent. Take away the unscented articles, then put your dog on leash. Place one scented article on the floor directly in front of the dog so she can reach it by lowering her head. Hold the leash in BOTH hands, low and close to your body. **Without moving your arms,** give the command you use for scent work. Follow the command with praise. If the dog starts, fine! There is no need for a correction. But the next time she may not. In that case, give one hard downward jerk on the leash with extra praise, then pick up the article and hand it to her unless, of course, she reaches for it herself. Repeat the correction as often as necessary, or until your dog will start when she hears the command. Give praise AFTER the command, whether you jerk the leash or not.

Alternate method: Hold the leash as described above but play it out until the loop that leads back to the dog's collar is four or five inches above the floor. If the dog doesn't start, stamp on the leash with the **left** foot, give praise, then pick up the article and hand it to her or encourage her to pick it up herself.

If your dog is still stubborn about retrieving scent articles, ask an assistant to face you and your dog, while holding the leash at its full length. Place the article between yourself and the assistant. Give the command and follow the command with praise. If the dog doesn't start, the assistant jerks the dog toward the article with ONE snap of the leash. You must then run forward, praise your dog, clap your hands in play, and encourage her to pick up the article. Apply leash corrections to the retrieving of all three scented articles, the unscented one, in the meantime, having been taken away. Leash corrections for failure to retrieve on command should never be made with the unscented articles scattered about. In her effort to get the article BEFORE the jerk on her collar, your dog will grab the first article she sees, even the wrong article.

When your dog will retrieve both articles on the first command while the leash is on, take the leash off, and if she performs perfectly, add the unscented articles, one at a time.

Dog Is Slow To Start For Articles

Same as **Doesn't Start On First Command**; but make a correction even though the dog starts by herself. A jerk on the collar when she doesn't expect it may snap her out of her lethargy.

Dog Retrieves Articles Slowly

Instead of **placing** the unscented articles, make a game of the scent work. Let your dog retrieve the articles in play. If this doesn't speed her up, try running after her and "spanking" her with your LEFT hand (if she is a big dog) or toss something at her heels (if she is a small dog). After she picks up the article, turn and RUN, or turn and clap your hands. Instinctively, the dog should speed up. If not, a cleverly disguised correction from the outside may help: Ask an assistant to toss something at the dog's heels while she is meandering toward you on the return, clap your hands and give extra praise to cover up the correction. If your dog is the scary type, avoid outside corrections.

Dog Grabs Any Article When Right Article Can't Be Found Quickly

Your dog won't panic if you train her to hunt for long periods of time. Place the scented article some distance away from the unscented ones and encourage her with "Keep looking! Keep looking!" When your dog finds that nothing happens when she takes an unusually long time to find the article, she will gain confidence.

Dog Runs Wild When Holding Scent Articles

If your dog starts tearing around, throw some object at her feet—a rolled magazine, your shoe, anything! Kneel, and use a demanding "COME!" Follow by coaxing, and when she comes, pat her.

SCENT DISCRIMINATION Problems—How To Overcome Them

Dog Comes Back Without The Article

Don't let your dog come back without the article you sent her for. Hold your leash rolled into a ball or hold a rolled magazine. If your dog starts back WITHOUT the scent article, throw what you are holding and block her. At the same time, run forward and encourage her to pick up the article you sent her for. Use a different numbered set of articles each time your dog works. This will train her to keep looking until she finds something with your scent.

Dog Takes The Wrong Article

Follow the suggestions for teaching SCENT DISCRIMINATION. Use the dog's favorite articles placed among "odds and ends." Gradually add articles that are similar, but keep the dog on leash so you can PULL her away if she tries to take the wrong one. Avoid yelling, and if the dog is working off leash, when she makes a mistake, quietly walk to her, pry open her mouth so she will drop the article, then give one jerk on the collar and encourage her to pick the correct one. Each time you practice, use different numbered articles.

Dog Stands Over Articles

A second command is what your dog is waiting for. Don't give it! Slowly walk to her, take hold of the ring of her collar and give it one jerk. Point to the scented article and say a demanding "TAKE THAT!" When she picks it up, run backward and give praise. The important thing is to make the correction with the collar BEFORE you give the second command.

Dog Doesn't Sniff Articles

Use the clip-board suggested earlier in training for SCENT DISCRIMINATION, or use the leash and jerk her head up when she reaches for the wrong one.

SCENT DISCRIMINATION Problems—How To Overcome Them

Dog Drops The Articles

If your dog drops the articles some distance away, use the same correction as for **Dog Stands Over Articles.** If she drops the articles at your feet, put the dog on leash, give her an article to hold, then walk backward while she follows in front. When you halt, command "Sit—stay!" Alternate this exercise with a series of comes at the length of the leash. Use the command "Sit—STAY!" each time the dog sits in front. If her head goes down, cuff her chin up and say "Hold it! Hold it!" If she drops what she is holding, slap her sharply on the nose BEFORE you pick up the article to make her try again.

When working off leash, just as your dog sits to deliver the articles, continue to use the verbal command "STAY!" Hearing the unexpected command should make her keep the article in her mouth.

Dog Mouths Articles

You may never cure your dog completely of mouthing, but if you follow these suggestions, she may mouth her articles less:

Use articles made of hard material.

Discourage jaw movement. Cuff your dog under the chin or warn her with "Easy! Easy!" each time she clamps down on objects she is holding.

Train your dog to carry breakable things, such as a raw egg or a small balloon. If what she is carrying breaks as the result of playing with it, she may learn to carry with gentleness.

If your dog is working off leash and she starts to mouth her articles, call out a loud "AAH!" or "NO!" When she holds without mouthing, praise and pat her.

Dog Won't Release Articles

Take hold of the article with one hand and command "OUT!" If your dog doesn't let go, slap her ONCE on the nose with your free hand. Praise and pat her AFTER she releases the article.

SCENT DISCRIMINATION Problems—How To Overcome Them

Alternate correction: Ask an assistant to hide behind a tree, a post, or a low wall. After your dog brings the article to you, command "Out!" If she starts a tug of war, the assistant throws something at the dog's feet to surprise her. The unexpected crash should make your dog release the article immediately. When she does, praise and pat her.

Dog Acts Uncertain On First Article

During practice, move to a new location after your dog retrieves the first article. Give her one chance to retrieve, then move a second time. If your dog doesn't receive more than one opportunity in the same location, she may become more confident about going out for the first scent article in strange surroundings.

If the cause of your dog's uncertainty is the SCENT DISCRIMINATION **command,** change commands. Your dog may have an unpleasant association with the words "Find it!" but will respond willingly to the command "Take it!" or "Get it!"

Dog Picks Up Dumbbell-Shaped Articles By Ends

Fasten a block of wood on each end of your practice articles, large enough so the dog can't get her mouth around them. Once she gets into the **habit** of picking up the articles by the centerpiece, gradually reduce the size of the blocks, then take them away entirely. When exhibiting in Obedience Trials, avoid touching the articles on the ends. Scent only the bar.

It is assumed that since your dog is being trained for SCENT DISCRIMINATION in the advanced UTILITY Course, she will have overcome such things as crooked sits, sloppy finishes and other problems that are point losers. If you are still bothered by "little things," consult **The Complete Novice Obedience Course** and **The Complete Open Obedience Course.** (Howell Book House.)

THE DIRECTED RETRIEVE

The only new thing about the DIRECTED RETRIEVE is the directional part. The retrieve is the same basic Retrieve on the Flat as in the Open exercises.

If the dog has not retrieved the glove before, teach her now. This can be done in the house on a rainy day. Make a game of it: show her the glove, toss it from one hand to the other, tease her to take it from your hand. If she shows no interest in the glove, put it in her mouth with praise. Take it from her and toss it on the ground and encourage her to get it. Since she is already retrieving the dumbbell, she will soon learn. Until she will retrieve the glove, there is no point in proceeding.

When she retrieves the glove willingly, and this is seldom a problem, leave her on a Sit-Stay and place the glove. Return to her and send her for the glove, giving the directional signal with the left hand. The directional signal is a swing forward ALONG the floor, not upward, but pointing at the glove, with the thumb up and the little finger toward the floor, the hand passing the dog's shoulder and beyond the dog's nose, as she starts after the glove. The knees may be bent but do not move the feet.

When she retrieves willingly and immediately on your signal and command, leave her on a Sit-Stay and place the glove at a 90-degree angle to the left of where your dog is sitting. Pivot 90 degrees and face the glove. As the dog becomes experienced the turn will become part of her signal as to which glove she is to retrieve. Therefore we exaggerate the turn, but send the dog straight to the glove. Give the signal and send her.

Practice on the pivot is a good exercise at this point. Going to the right around the handler to heel position is not permitted by the rules in this exercise, so the dog that has been taught to go to heel in this manner must be retaught as a new exercise. A different command from the one used for the regular going to heel command will prevent confusion for these dogs. Some suggestions for this different command are "Turn!" or "Place!"

Do the exercise on a right 90-degree turn. Praise your dog lavishly, when she starts, when she reaches the glove, when she picks it up, and when she returns. Gradually drop the praise in the same sequence until she finally gets praise only when she has finished the exercise. Send her on a straight retrieve.

Do not work too long at this exercise at a time. Avoid boring your dog. Stop after a good performance. But if corrections have been necessary throughout the practice session, do an exercise she does well and praise her for her good work.

Up to this time, no other glove has been evident for your dog to retrieve. The next time you work your dog, place the left and right hand gloves at a 60-degree angle. Send your dog to each glove. Place the center glove and send your dog.

Have the instructor place all three gloves, the outside gloves at a 60-degree angle, and the third glove directly in front. Have her drop the center glove last. Send your dog for the center glove. Have the center glove replaced. Send your dog for one of the side gloves. If she retrieves the proper glove, praise her; if she starts towards the wrong glove, the instructor, standing behind the center glove, points toward the proper glove, and the handler encourages her with "Good girl!" When she is retrieving the proper glove each time, the gloves are placed in their Obedience ring position, the outer gloves at a 45-degree angle and the third glove in the center.

Do not be afraid to go back in your training if the dog seems confused or uncertain, even to the extent of tossing the glove out for a retrieve or two.

Make a game of the Directed Retrieve. Drop an article surreptitiously and walk a few yards, then about-turn and give the signal and command to retrieve. Be sure the article is in plain sight. Drop two articles 10 or 12 feet apart, swing abreast of the articles and stop some 15 feet away and directly opposite one article. Send her first for one article, and then the other. This will provide practice in areas other than the regular training grounds.

If you have a dog that retrieves eagerly and takes corrections well, which you will know by the time you have reached the Utility stage of training, there are short-cuts to the teaching of the DIRECTED RE-TRIEVE.

Place the right and center gloves in position. With the dog at heel position, make a 45-degree turn to the left. Toss out the glove giving the command and signal to retrieve. Repeat, making any necessary corrections, with praise. **Place** the glove and send her.

Repeat the exercise with the center glove. If she starts for the wrong glove, reprimand with a "NO!" or "PHOOEY!" and direct her to the proper glove. Be sure your signal is **along** the floor toward the glove. And don't forget the praise!

Have the instructor place the gloves. The instructor should stand behind the line of gloves to block the dog and point to the proper article if the dog starts toward the wrong glove. A line affixed between two chairs at the dog's shoulder height can be used as a guide for the dog. When sending the dog for the left-hand glove, one chair should be placed behind and to the right of the glove, and the other to the right of the handler. For the right-hand glove, place one chair behind and to the left of the glove, and the other to the left of the handler.

From this point on it is practise, practise, practise. Praise with every correction.

Things To Remember When Teaching THE DIRECTED RETRIEVE

Give the proper signal for the Directed Retrieve, moving the left hand along the floor, past the dog's shoulder and nose, **toward** the glove, NOT up in the air. The knees may be bent to bring the hand on a level with the dog's eyes, but do not move the feet.

Praise with every correction. Corrections without simultaneous praise are worse than no corrections at all.

Do not work your dog at this exercise too long at a time. Avoid boring her. Stop after a good performance. Or, if corrections have been necessary throughout the practice session, do an exercise she does well and praise her for her good work before ending the training session.

If you must make severe corrections on the Retrieve on the Flat parts of this exercise, make them on a dumbbell retrieve. Then do the retrieve with the glove, giving praise at the parts of the exercise where you gave praise with corrections when using the dumbbell, but avoiding the severe corrections with the glove.

DIRECTED RETRIEVE Problems—How To Overcome Them

Dog Does Not Make Change To Proper Heel Position When Handler Turns To Right Or Left

In practice, hold the leash wadded into a ball in your left hand, with just enough slack so there is a little loop at the collar. With the dog at heel position do a series of:
1. Steps to the right.
2. Quarter-turn pivots to the left.
3. About turns from a standstill.
4. A step to the rear.
5. Quarter-turn pivots to the right.

With each change of position, command "Heel!" Then snap the leash to make the dog assume the proper position. Give praise as you snap the leash. Reduce the Quarter-turn pivots to 45 degrees.

Dog Does Not Start On First Command

Since the signal is a part of this exercise, tie a short loop of rope through the collar, give the command and grab the loop, jerking the dog forward with praise as you give the signal.

Dog Does Not Go To Proper Glove

Try making the distance for the retrieve very short at first. Gradually increase the distance until the dog is retrieving at obedience trial distance.

There are several ways to keep the dog from veering away from the retrieve of the proper glove. A row of plumbing plungers or dowels connected with rope level to the dog's shoulder, and stretched from the handler to the glove, will help.

A 15-foot rope, fastened to the dog's collar, can be held by the instructor, who stands halfway between the dog and the handler and the glove, but to the outside of the path travelled by the dog. The rope is jerked only if the dog starts toward the wrong glove. The handler repeats the command with praise. For the center glove the instructor would stand behind the glove.

Dog Plays With Or Shakes Glove

Calling the dog immediately after she picks up the glove will aid in preventing the dog from playing with or shaking the glove. She cannot run and shake at the same time. Try giving her other soft objects, such as a soft cotton strip of cloth or a sock. If she shakes it, reprimand her and cuff her nose, saying "Stop that!"

THE SIGNAL EXERCISE

If you have trained your dog to stand-at-heel, to lie down, to sit from a down, to come when called and to go-to-heel position as outlined in **The Complete Novice Obedience Course** and **The Complete Open Obedience Course,** the SIGNAL EXERCISE will not be difficult.

Hold the leash in your right hand. Motion forward with your LEFT hand and start walking. Follow the signal with "Good Girl!" While moving forward, switch the leash to your left hand and signal the STAND with your RIGHT hand, or do it without changing the leash. When you give the signal, give additional praise. If your dog sits instead of standing, forget about the rest of the SIGNAL EXERCISE until you teach your dog to stand on signal. Keep the leash fastened to the dog's collar, then loop the handle end under her stomach. Hold the center of the leash in your LEFT hand. While walking, place your RIGHT hand with the leash in it in front of your dog's muzzle, which is the signal to stand. **Don't move your LEFT hand** unless your dog starts to sit. If she does, pull up on the leash to keep her in a standing position, and give praise. The RIGHT hand moves only if the dog creeps, in which case, bump her nose. The best way to impress upon your dog that she must not step forward after you signal the stand, is to cuff her nose once or twice with the hand that gives the signal.

Signal the STAY with your LEFT hand, and give the signal before you move your feet. Just as you step out on the right foot, cuff

The easy way to teach the STAND signal.

To overcome creeping, pull the leash taut.
If the dog moves, tap her under the chin.

your dog gently on the nose with your LEFT hand and she will have greater respect for the STAY signal. Let her remain standing for a few minutes while you face her, then circle back to heel position. Give the STAY signal a second time, face your dog, then signal the DOWN. The owner will be more successful with this signal if he will teach his dog to lie down when the hand is raised. This type of signal is easily seen at a distance and the dog will not be confused between the signal to lie down and the signal to COME, usually given by lowering the hand. Still more important, some judges consider the up-and-down motion a double signal. In an Obedience Trial, your dog could either fail or receive a penalty.

When you raise your hand for the DOWN signal, follow the signal with praise. If your dog doesn't go down at once or is slow to respond, stamp on the leash or bump the dog's nose ONCE with the signal hand. Keep fingers pointing **up**. Give praise with either correction and after the dog goes down, circle back to heel position and pat her. Signal the STAY, then face her, but not to the full length of the leash. Stand close enough so you can touch the dog's paws without taking steps. Signal the SIT. This is a backward, then forward, motion with the RIGHT hand (LEFT if you prefer), stopping on line with the body. If your dog hasn't jumped to a sitting position by the time your hand has stopped moving, reach out and tap her paws lightly with your foot. At the same time give an upward jerk on the leash. If you time your corrections properly, your dog should start to get up when your hand moves backward, and she should be sitting by the time the hand has come forward and is on line with your body. The palm of the hand is held toward the dog at all times, and praise is given with the signal.

Tell your dog "Stay!" and back to the full length of the leash. Signal the COME with a great deal of praise. Make a sweeping motion toward your body with either hand, but don't use both. Your dog should start when the hand moves. If she doesn't, drop your hand onto the leash with force and snap her toward you. Give praise and pat her after she is sitting in front. If she comes without the jerk on the leash, give praise just the same.

The final signal is the FINISH. Make a slight motion to your left side with your left hand if your dog is trained to go to the left. Use the right hand if the dog passes in back of you to go to heel position. If the FINISH signal is ignored, grab the leash with the signal hand and make a quick correction. Give praise while your dog is moving around to your side, whether you used the leash or not.

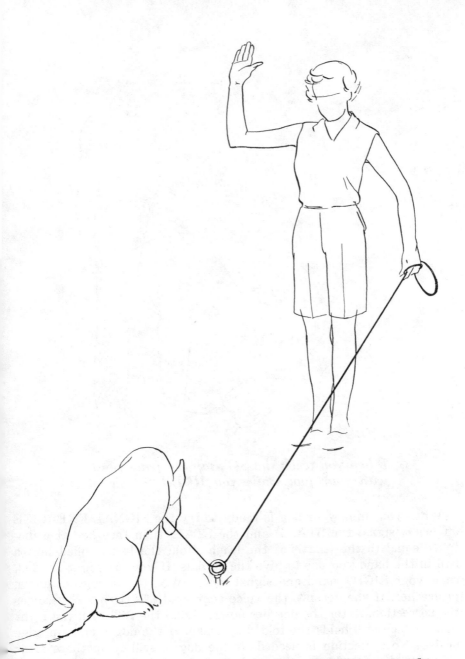

One of the many ways to teach your dog to DOWN on signal.

*When you teach the SIT, tap the paws gently
with your foot while you HOLD the signal.*

When you think your dog is ready to try the SIGNAL EXERCISE off leash, signal the STAND and the STAY, then face her at a distance equal to the length of the leash. Hold the leash rolled into a ball in the hand you use to give the signals. If you are right-handed, raise your RIGHT hand and signal the DOWN. If the dog lies down, praise her. If she doesn't, the voice command of "DOWN!" becomes the correction. After the dog lies down, signal the SIT with the right hand, which still holds the folded up leash. If the dog jumps up, give praise! No correction is needed. If the dog is still lying there after you give the signal, toss the leash underhanded, so it slides against her paws. At the same time, give a forceful command "SIT!" and move toward her.

Use ONE arm for the COME.

The COME signal and the signal to FINISH cause the least trouble in the SIGNAL EXERCISE. In any case, follow both signals with praise; and when you praise, be sincere!

Gradually increase the distance you stand away for the SIGNAL EXERCISE, but only if your dog obeys the **first** signal for all parts of the SIGNAL exercises, especially the DOWN and the SIT. When exhibiting in an Obedience Trial, an exhibitor can give a signal only once. Instead of repeating signals in practice, give effective correction after the first signal.

Things To Remember When Teaching The SIGNAL EXERCISE

While your dog is learning, keep her on leash, and stand CLOSE so you can make corrections without taking steps.

Give praise with every signal. Flattery can be dropped **after** your dog is trained, but praise disguises necessary correction and reassures the dog if she feels uncertain about a particular signal.

Give no more than one signal for each part of the exercise. If your dog doesn't obey the first signal, make a sharp correction with extra praise. When possible, make a correction or give the verbal command while the signal hand is held in position.

Follow no set pattern. When your dog doesn't know what is coming next, she will be less apt to anticipate your hand motions.

Give your dog every advantage by keeping signals distinct. Ask others to criticize your hand motions.

When the dog is working off leash and fails to obey a signal, use voice commands as a form of correction. Make the command a forceful one.

When you give signals, hold your arm so it doesn't visually blend into your body from a distance, and wait for your dog to look at you before you give a signal.

SIGNAL EXERCISE Problems—How To Overcome Them

Dog Doesn't Heel On Signal

Ask someone to stand directly behind your dog. Give the signal and follow the signal with praise. If the dog doesn't start, the assistant taps the dog on the hindquarters while you give extra praise. Halt, then repeat the exercise.

Dog Sits When Signalled To Stand

See SIGNAL EXERCISE, page 26 for ON-leash training. It is especially important that you give the signal to STAND while you and the dog are **both** moving forward.

Alternate correction: An assistant walks at the dog's left and slightly in back, with the leash looped under the dog's stomach. The owner gives the signal to stand, using his RIGHT hand. If the dog starts to sit down, the assistant gently lifts the dog to a standing position by pulling up on the leash. This correction is especially effective with small dogs that sit very quickly.

One way to correct the dog that sits when signalled to stand.

SIGNAL EXERCISE Problems—How To Overcome Them

Dog Doesn't Lie Down On Signal

See SIGNAL EXERCISE, page 26 for ON-leash training.

Alternate correction, with the dog off leash and at a distance: Hold a small, rolled magazine along the palm and wrist of the hand you use to give the signal. After you raise your hand, hold it a moment and if your dog doesn't lie down, toss the magazine overhanded, so that it lands in front of the dog. With your hand still raised, command "DOWN!"

Dog Doesn't Sit From The Down

See SIGNAL EXERCISE, page 26 for ON-leash correction.

Alternate correction, with the dog off leash and at a distance: Hold the rolled magazine along the palm and wrist of the signal hand. Move your hand backward, then forward, for the signal to SIT. If your dog isn't sitting by the time your hand is at your side, toss the magazine underhanded, so that it slides under the dog, then run forward and give a forceful command of "SIT!" When the dog is sitting, pat her.

Alternate correction: Ask an assistant to hold the end of a long line and to stand out of sight in back of the dog. When the dog ignores the signal to sit, the assistant jerks the leash backward and upward, while the owner gives praise. The line can be run through wire fencing or a pulley, and the assistant can stand off to one side, but the jerk on the line must be upward as well as backward in order to pull the dog **up**.

The assistant can make corrections for both the DOWN and the SIT by standing close to the dog and using the leash to make the dog perform each exercise. The owner gives the signals and the assistant forces the dog to obey. Both owner and assistant give praise.

Dog Doesn't Come On Signal

See SIGNAL EXERCISE, page 26 for ON-leash correction.

For off-leash correction, ask an assistant to hide so as to be in back of the dog when you leave her. Give the signal to come, and follow it with sincere praise. If the dog starts, the assistant does nothing. If she doesn't, ask the assistant to toss something or make a noise. Give extra praise, turn your back and clap your hands, or

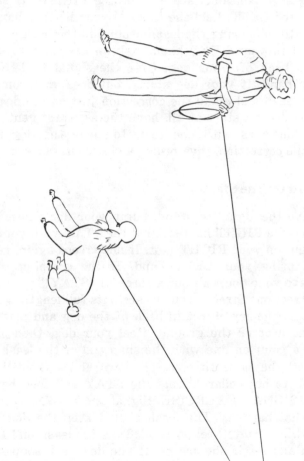

Correcting the dog that won't sit at a distance.

turn and run! This encouragement will help your dog to forget the outside correction. If your dog is not afraid of people, the assistant can stand directly behind your dog and if she doesn't start, tap her with one foot.

Dog Doesn't Finish On Signal

Put your dog on leash, and face her for the FINISH. If she is trained to go to the LEFT, hold the leash in your RIGHT hand. If she goes to the RIGHT, bring the leash around to the back of your body and hold it in your LEFT hand. Ask an assistant to stand close to, and in back of, your dog. Give the signal to FINISH, using your free hand. If your dog starts, but does an incomplete finish, grab the leash and make the correction just as the dog sits down. If the dog doesn't start at all, have the assistant gently tap your dog's hindquarters with one foot, to make the dog move around. After the correction, give praise and encouragement.

Dog Moves Forward On The Stand

After you give the signal to stand, bump your dog's nose with the signal hand—the RIGHT hand. Signal the STAY with your left hand and step out on your RIGHT foot. If she creeps again, repeat the correction, using your LEFT hand. If the creeping occurs AFTER you leave your dog, call out a forceful "STAY!"

Alternate correction: Stretch your leash to its full length. Fasten the handle to a stationary object in back of the dog and place the snap end on the floor or the ground. Heel your dog, then signal the STAND at a point on line with the snap end of the leash. Pat your dog, and at the same time, reach down and surreptitiously fasten the leash to her collar. Signal the STAY and face her for the rest of the SIGNAL EXERCISE. Signal the DOWN, then the SIT, and see what happens. The leash should keep the dog from moving forward. Return to heel position. Take the leash off! Leave your dog again and see if she creeps. If she does, ask someone to hold the handle of the leash, and to jerk the dog backward when she moves forward.

SIGNAL EXERCISE Problems—How To Overcome Them

Dog Anticipates The Down

Signal your dog to STAND. Leave her, face her for the DOWN, then turn and walk away. If she starts to lie down without a signal, call out "STAY!" Return to where you were originally standing, wait a few moments, then return to heel position.

In practice, follow no definite pattern.

Dog Anticipates The Sit Signal

Signal your dog to lie down. Wait, then turn and walk away. If she starts to get up without permission call out "DOWN! STAY!" Return to where you were originally standing, wait, then go back to heel position.

In practice, follow no definite pattern.

Dog Moves Forward On The Sit Signal

Break the **habit** of creeping. Put your dog on leash. Stand close! Give the signal to SIT and if the dog moves forward, lift your knee (if she is a big dog) and bump her chest. If she is a small dog, use the side of your foot and push her backward. The important thing is to let the dog START to creep and then correct her.

Dog Anticipates The Come Signal

Signal the STAND, the DOWN, the SIT, then signal the DOWN again. If your dog, thinking you made a mistake, starts to come, call out a demanding "DOWN!" Signal the SIT, then go back to your dog and pat her.

Dog Anticipates The Signal To Finish

Don't let your dog FINISH every time you call her. Pivot on your left foot, and step back to heel position yourself. If the dog moves when you move, tell her emphatically "Stay!"

Dog Drops Only Halfway

See correction: **Dog Anticipates The Sit Signal.**

SIGNAL EXERCISE Problems—How To Overcome Them

Dog Looks Away During Signal Exercise

During practice, every time your dog looks away, make a noise such as "Sh-h-h!" or call out "Hey!" A toy water gun may be effective if your dog persistently ignores you.

Dog Comes From Down Without Sitting

See correction: **Dog Moves Forward On The Sit Signal.**

When you increase the distance you stand from your dog, fasten the handle of the leash to a stationary object in back of her so she can't come forward. When you take the leash off, **run** toward her or toss something to block her if she moves toward you.

Dog Creeps On All Parts Of The Signal Exercise

Put your dog on leash. Signal the STAND. Face your dog! Tighten the leash gradually, and try to "pull" her forward. If she moves, bump her nose and demand "STAY!" then pat her or tousle her ear with the hand you used to correct her.

Do the same with the DOWN and the SIT. Correct all FORWARD movement except the COME part of the exercise. Gradually increase the distance you stand but fasten the handle of the leash to a stationary object in back of the dog. After you leave her, signal the DOWN and the SIT, then return to your dog and pat her. The leash, which acts as a checkrein, may help break the habit of creeping.

Dog Loses Points On Heeling

See: FREE HEELING (The Complete Open Obedience Course)

Dog Responds To The COME Signal, But Comes Slowly

During training, signal the COME, then turn your back, clap your hands and give praise. After your dog gets into the habit of coming, gradually eliminate the turning away and the clapping, but continue the praise, postponing it each time you call your dog, to the point where she has completed the exercise and has gone to heel position. Offer food if she likes to eat.

If your dog creeps, put her on leash,
then BLOCK all forward movement.

DIRECTED JUMPING

For the purpose of teaching the DIRECTED JUMPING and offering suggestions on how to overcome problems, this exercise is divided into two parts: (1) **The Directed Go,** and (2) **The Directed Jump.** It is suggested that owners make no attempt to combine the GO with the JUMP to make the completed DIRECTED JUMPING exercise until their dogs are thoroughly familiar with each.

The Directed Go

As suggested earlier, when owners **prepare** their dogs for the Utility Course, the advanced exercises are more easily taught. Apply early training to the Directed Go through games. If your dog likes to play ball, wave your hand toward her and say **"GO** back! GO back!" If she backs away, then stops, say it again and keep repeating the words until she moves some distance away. Toss her the ball, then have her bring it to you so you can make her "Go back!" again.

If your dog is the greedy type, place her dinner on the other side of the room or across the training area. Return to her and say "GO! Dinner!" with emphasis on the GO. Make a game of placing your rolled-up leash on the opposite side of the training yard, then tell your dog "Go! Leash!" This command can later be changed to the "Go! Sit!" required in Obedience Trials.

40

Another method is to put your dog on leash, say "GO!" and encourage her to lead the way to the opposite end of the training yard. While she is still moving away from you, call her name and when she turns around, say "Sit!" Pat her or give her something to eat, lead her back, and send her again. Still another way is to send your dog from one person to another. One person says "GO!" the other says "Come!" Each in turn makes the dog sit, then rewards her with food (if she likes to eat) or a generous pat. This preliminary training makes a dog associate something pleasant with the word "GO!" and when the line and pulley are used to teach the DIRECTED JUMPING exercise, the dog will take to them more kindly.

To teach the DIRECTED GO methodically, secure one hundred feet of light-weight plastic or nylon clothesline and a covered-type pulley. Cut off a two-foot length of line that you can use to tie the pulley to a fence, post, tree, or stake, or to a ring on the side of a building. Put a snap on one end of the remaining line, and make the other end into a looped handle.

The majority of dogs respond to the line willingly and with spirit, **when the line is used the right way.** Through its use it is possible to train systematically and give effective corrections, thus making the dog reliable in a short length of time. It is suggested that owners **try** the line as described on the following pages. If they find that their dog is one of the few that shows fear, possibly because of some former unpleasant association with a rope, or because the dog is the panicky type, the other suggested methods for teaching a dog to GO will then have to be used.

For the first few lessons of the GO, select a long, narrow passageway in which to do the training so that your dog will get into the habit of going in a straight line. This can be a roadway, a strip of land between two fences, or a long, narrow hallway. Ask an assistant to help (you will need help later on, anyway) to get the dog off to a good start. Snap the line to your dog's collar and make her sit at heel position, facing the pulley, yet not too far away. Your dog must first learn to GO a short distance before you send her the required length. The assistant pulls the line while you walk or run **with** your dog. Hold the line in your LEFT hand and say "Go! Good Girl. Good Girl." When you reach the stopping point, back up quickly, command "Robin, Sit!" then reward her with a pat. Take the dog back to the starting point, and do this again. When a dog balks at the line or shows fear, it is usually the result of seeing the line for the first time

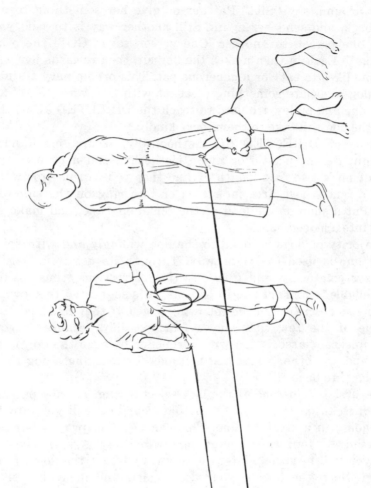

GO with your dog the first time you put her on line.

and not understanding it, or hearing the mysterious squeak of the pulley. If your dog has company on her "maiden voyage" she will gain confidence and be unafraid. The assistant, when pulling the line, should stand off to one side of the training yard or in back of the owner, to keep the dog from being suspicious of the assistant's actions.

Run with your dog on the GO until she shows no fear of the line, then start "dropping behind." In other words, start with the dog, then slow to a walk and let the line pull the dog outward. The important things are to give **constant praise** while the dog is being taken out on the line, and to reward her after she is sitting. Use whatever means she likes best, food, praise, a pat, or a ball to chase. Then take her by the collar, lead her back, and do the exercise again.

Every time the exercise is repeated, the drag on the line will get lighter. The dog may have braced herself in the beginning, but she will start treading gingerly toward the pulley if the assistant uses a **gentle steady** pull on the line and the owner **encourages** the dog every step of the way. Don't forget the extra reward when the dog sits on command after the GO.

There are differences of opinion as to whether the arm signal should be used with the GO command. My personal feeling is that it should not. The giving of direction with the arm is understandable in Field Trial work because no jumps are involved, but in the DIRECTED JUMPING exercise, the arm is used to indicate the jump the dog must take. Hand motion on the GO could cause the dog to be confused between the GO and the JUMP. My preference is to use the dog's name with the command "GO!" and since all Obedience rings are set up with the Solid Hurdle on one side and the Bar on the other, the dog quickly learns that she must pass BETWEEN the jumps on the way out but NEVER on the way back. If the owner prefers to use his arm on the GO, the arm closest to the dog is the logical one.

When your dog has learned to move out on the line without fighting it, handle the line yourself. Hold the end of the line after it doubles back from the pulley. With your dog sitting at heel position, calmly give the command "Robin, GO!" and make it a happy command. In fact, all GO commands should be given in a gay, cheerful voice. After you give the command, walk slowly BACKWARD and pull gently on the line to take your dog in the opposite direction. Encourage her with "GO. Good Girl! GO. Good Girl!" and if she braces herself, continue to pull slowly, with praise. After she has

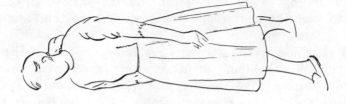

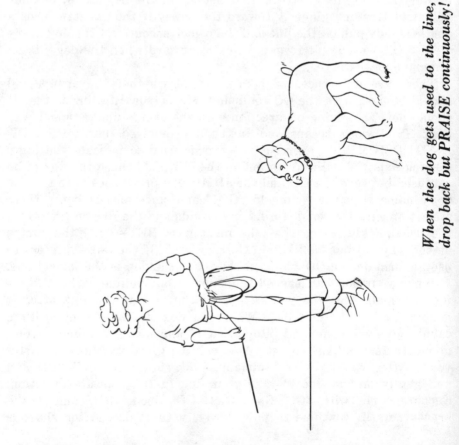

When the dog gets used to the line,
drop back but PRAISE continuously!

moved out a few feet, even though you did most of the work, call her by name to encourage her to turn around, then say "Sit!" and give the line a tug. If the pulley is higher than the dog's head, the upward jerk of the line will help to make the dog sit, just as it did in basic training. However, any backward tug accompanied by the command "Sit" should get results. When you tug on the line, say another "Good Girl!" then throw her the ball for her to catch, or walk to her and pat her or give her a tasty morsel.

When you move to the training yard, set the jumps in place so the dog will get accustomed to going between the hurdles. Design a narrow passageway so your dog will learn to GO in a straight line. Stretch two pieces of rope or two strips of low fencing. Sometimes a rubber runner is sufficient encouragement to get dogs into the habit of going out straight, especially dogs trained indoors. They prefer to walk on a runner rather than on the slippery floor. After your dog knows to what point she must go, take away the "aisle" so she won't depend upon it for guidance.

During each practice session, start the lesson by sending the dog just a few feet. After each successful GO, increase the distance. The ultimate goal, naturally, is the distance required in Obedience Trials.

The way you use the line and the timing of commands with corrections are what make training on the pulley a success. Give the first "Robin, Go!" BEFORE you tug on the line. If the dog starts, then slows down or stops entirely, repeat the "GO!" without using the dog's name, and say it demandingly, after which, tug on the line a second time. Repeat this action every time your dog stops without permission. If you work with an assistant, make certain the assistant waits until you give the commands before jerking the line. While your dog is still moving away, call out a cheerful "Robin!—SIT!" Follow with "Good Girl!" If you pause after you call the dog's name and before you give the command, she will turn more completely to face you. After she is sitting, toss a ball for her to catch (if she likes to play ball), or walk to her and give her a pat or something to eat.

The DIRECTED JUMPING is the one Obedience exercise in which your dog must leave you for no apparent reason. To overcome uncertainty, make the dog understand she must GO and SIT at the opposite end of the field before you will throw her a ball to catch or before she receives the cracker or dog candy she anticipates. Later on, jumping the hurdles can be her reward for the "GO," because most dogs enjoy, and understand, this part of the exercise.

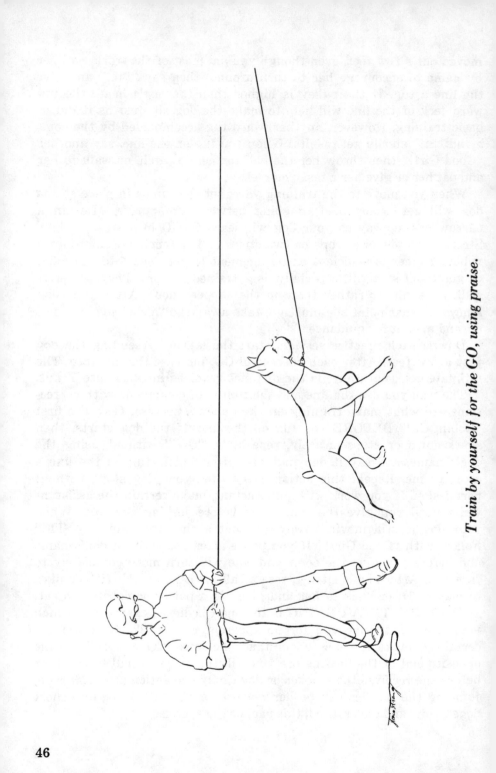

Train by yourself for the GO, using praise.

Another way to teach your dog that GO means the opposite of COME, is to leave her sitting on the center line between the two jumps, with her back to the pulley. Fasten the line to her collar, BACK away, and face her across the field. Hold the line or have the assistant hold it; then, from the distance, command "GO!" without using the dog's name. Chances are she will start toward you, thinking you made a mistake and meant for her to come. If she does, or if she continues to just sit, give one tug on the line, then encourage her to GO as you reel in the line. Even at a distance, when a dog hears the word "GO!" she should turn and move **away** from the person who gave the command, but this comes only with practice.

While training your dog to do the GO exercise, never let her stop of her own free will. Keep her going outward until you call her name. When she turns, tell her "Sit!"

Your next step is to unsnap the line from the collar while the dog is sitting at heel position, and place the line on the ground, close to the dog. This will be a test to show how well you used the line while training. Do a short GO at first. Give the single command "Robin, GO!" with continuous praise, and see what happens. If she surprises you and goes all the way, call out cheerfully "Robin, Sit!" With the line no longer attached to the collar, a second command "STAY!" will discourage her from coming back to you. In the meantime, while your dog is moving away, back up and pull the line so the snap end moves out with the dog. It might be better, in this case, to have an assistant pull the line so the dog won't be disturbed by movements in back of her. When she has gone far enough, stop her, walk to her, pat her, and give her a reward.

If, instead of going all the way, she stops, **don't say anything,** except a quiet "Stay!" Then slowly walk out to her, snap the line on her collar, say "Stay!" again, and go back to your original position, which is facing her across the training yard. **From the distance,** call out a forceful "GO!" then give the line one good tug, or have your assistant do it. When your dog is again sitting at the opposite end of the field, give her a reward, lead her back to the starting point, unsnap the line and try again. Repeat the SAME correction when necessary.

From this point on, it is practice and more practice. Send your dog in the opposite direction. Send her **across** the training yard instead of the length of it. Make her do the GO into a blank wall, and again in wide open spaces. And under no circumstances send your dog in a new

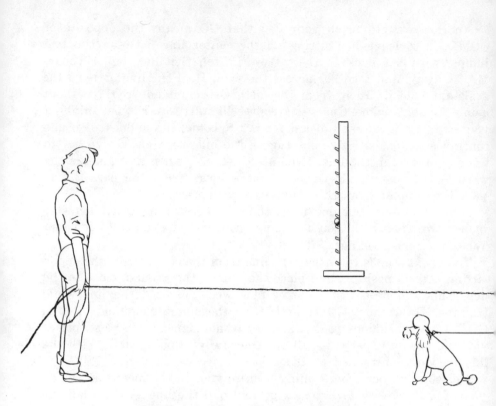

*Teach your dog that GO means to GO
AWAY. Send her from a distance.*

location without having the line and pulley set in place, ready for a correction. The reason so many dogs fail the DIRECTED JUMPING exercise in Obedience Trials is that the dogs are trained in one special area and when they are asked to leave the owner amid strange surroundings at a dog show, their reaction is one of uncertainty or confusion. They stop before they are told, or the distance they go is too short to allow for the jumping.

Things To Remember When Teaching The DIRECTED GO

Say your dog's name and give the command "GO!" in preference to using a signal. If you give a signal, use the left arm.

Give the GO command in a HAPPY tone of voice.

Hold the line in your left hand and, while an assistant pulls the line to take up the slack, **walk** or **run** with your dog until she gets used to the line and the pulley.

Later, let go of the line with your left hand, walk with the dog but let the assistant pull the dog out.

Still later, start dropping back. **Start** with the dog, then slow up or stop entirely while the dog continues to move away from you on line.

Give the GO command before using the line, either to start the dog or to correct her for stopping too soon.

Give constant praise while your dog is moving away from you.

When your dog has gone the full distance, call her name loudly and cheerfully. After she turns, tell her "SIT!" Reward her!

If she is not on line, follow the sit command with "STAY!" which can be dropped later.

If your dog is working off leash and she stops without permission, tell her quietly "Stay!" then walk to her, snap the line on her collar, back away, tell her "GO!" and make the correction at the point she stopped.

Practice in strange surroundings with the line and pulley set in place. If suddenly you fail to make progress, go back and start at the beginning.

DIRECTED GO Problems—How To Overcome Them

Dog Balks At The Line Unless Owner Goes With The Dog

Shorten the distance you stand from the pulley to about twelve or fourteen feet. Without moving your feet, command "Robin, Go!" Follow with "Good Girl! Good Girl!" while an assistant, **slowly** and **gently,** pulls the dog forward. Dragging the dog three or four feet should overcome obstinacy, but the owner must give constant praise. Be extra enthusiastic when the dog takes a few steps by herself.

Alternate suggestion: If your dog likes to play ball, take the line off for the time being, and roll a ball to the far end of the field and say "Robin, Go!" Let her chase it and after she picks up the ball, tell her "Sit!" At first, let her go for the ball without waiting. Later, hold her by the collar until the ball stops rolling, then give the command. When she will chase the ball willingly and cheerfully, attach the line to her collar and let her drag it while she chases the ball. Later, an assistant, very gently, takes up the slack.

Dog Doesn't Start On Command

Put your dog on line and have her sit at heel position, about ten feet from the pulley. Give the command "Robin, GO!" and follow the command with "Good Girl!" Don't give her a chance to refuse to start. Jerk the line immediately after the word "GO!" or have an assistant do it for you, then run forward in a playful manner. Repeat three or four times, then give the command and praise WITHOUT jerking the line.

When the leash is off, give the command and while you are saying the "Good Girl!" reach back with your RIGHT foot and tap the dog's rear. Rush forward with her after she starts, make her sit, then give praise.

If the "kickback" fails to do the trick, ask two or three people to stand in back of your dog, and, if she still doesn't start, to stamp their feet or slide something toward her to make her move, after which you must run with her to the opposite end of the training area. If your dog is afraid of people, avoid outside corrections.

DIRECTED GO Problems—How To Overcome Them

Dog Stops Before She Is Told

Don't give a second command. Walk to your dog, snap the line on her collar and tell her "Stay!" Go back to your original position, and from the distance, command "GO!" and jerk the leash once, giving praise. If no line is available, chase her or toss something at her heels in a playful manner, in such a way that she will continue to move outward.

Dog Takes Jumps On The Way Out

Remove temptation! Leave the jump uprights in place but take away the bar and the solid boards. Later, place the bar and the boards in position but leave them on the ground.

To correct the dog that persistently jumps the hurdles going out, ask two assistants to stand in back of you, but off to the side. One assistant stands in line with the Solid Hurdle and the other in line with the Bar. If the dog starts toward either jump instead of going between them, the assistant on whichever side the dog is headed, tosses something in front of the jump to block the dog from jumping. The owner then runs forward and encourages the dog to go between the jumps. Timing is important. The thrown object must arrive at the jump early enough to keep the dog from jumping, but not so early as to affect the GO part of the exercise. If they prefer, the assistants can stand at the outside corners of the hurdles and block the dog by running in.

Dog Doesn't Go In A Straight Line

See DIRECTED GO, page 41, for training.

For off-leash correction, have two assistants stand, one on each side of the training area. After the dog passes between the jumps and starts to veer toward one side or another, the assistant drops or tosses some object to make the dog stay on the center line. Take care not to frighten or confuse the dog with too sharp a correction.

DIRECTED GO Problems—How To Overcome Them

Dog Remains Standing When Commanded To Sit

Put your dog on line and do a short GO of eight or ten feet. Command the dog to sit, then jerk the line without waiting. In this case the pulley must be above the dog's head in order to get an upward pull that will make the dog sit. After several hard corrections without waiting for the dog to sit of her own accord, try it without the leash. Use a forceful command and at the same time, give the dog the signal to sit. If she is still slow to sit, bang on something or have an assistant do it for you. The unexpected loud noise is especially effective for the dog that returns to the owner without jumping or jumps without waiting for a signal.

Dog Creeps When Told To Sit

Put your dog on leash, and correct as you did for creeping on signals. Stand close to your dog. If she comes forward when she gets up from the down, or when she sits or lies down from the stand, lift your knee (if she is a large dog), or use the inside of your foot (for the small dog), and bump her to make her back up.

When working off leash, after you send your dog, call her by name, then tell her "SIT! STAY!" The stay command is one she has heard all her life. If she is obedient, she should hold her position. If she doesn't, run forward, bump her, and make her move back. An alternate suggestion is for you to hold a small, rolled magazine and when she creeps, to throw it and block her.

The Directed Jump

Owners can practice their dogs on the DIRECTED GO and the DIRECTED JUMP at the same time, **providing they make no attempt to combine the two exercises.** A dog should be thoroughly reliable in each before the two parts are put together.

With the jumps set in place and kept at half their normal height, leave your dog on a sit-stay in front of the Solid Hurdle, approximately ten to fifteen feet away. Face her at an equal distance on the opposite side of the hurdle, but stand nearer the center of the ring. If your dog is to go to the right, raise your RIGHT arm and hold it on line with your body, parallel to the ground. As you raise your arm, say "Jump! Good Girl!" If she leaps on command, give extra praise. If she remains sitting, run forward, pat the top board with the SIGNAL hand, and encourage the dog to jump.

Next, leave her sitting facing the hurdle in the opposite direction, while you back away and prepare to give the signal with your LEFT arm, to make her jump to your left. Raise your arm from your side, again holding it on line with your body and parallel to the ground. Again, command "Jump! Good Girl!"

If your dog will leap the Solid Hurdle when you motion with either hand, do the same using the Bar Jump. Place the bar low so the dog won't be tempted to go under. Avoid mistakes until your dog knows what is expected of her and you won't have to correct so often. If you taught your dog to jump a black and white jumping stick (as outlined in **The Complete Novice Obedience Course)** you should have little trouble with the Bar Hurdle.

Each time you practice, move your dog back from the jump two or three feet. Do this gradually until you reach the twenty-foot distance required in Obedience Trials. Also, work more toward the center of the ring so your dog will learn to detour before jumping. As you progress, it would be unusual if your dog at no time made an attempt to pass between the hurdles. When she does, don't try to block the dog by running toward **her.** Run to the **jump** you signalled, instead. In passing between the hurdles, your dog is only trying to get to you. If you move toward the jump, she will change her course and go with you. You can then encourage her to leap the hurdle by patting the top board or the bar with the hand you used to give the signal.

As the training progresses, ask an assistant to stand in the center of the ring, on line with the two jumps. The fact that someone is blocking the way will help make your dog circle before jumping, especially if you ask the assistant to raise one arm and point to the jump when you raise yours. Any attempt to pass between the jumps is blocked by both owner and assistant running toward the hurdle the dog was **supposed** to jump. Both owner and assistant give praise. As your dog becomes reliable, the assistant moves toward the outside of the ring, finally leaving it entirely.

As soon as you can, stop using the jumping command when you give the signal to start your dog. If she isn't watching and suddenly hears you order her to jump, she may start but take the wrong hurdle. Instead, raise your arm for the signal and follow by saying "Good Girl!" This will teach your dog to START on signal but, more important, it teaches her to TAKE DIRECTION before she starts. If you **must** use a voice command, say it AFTER your arm is in place and AFTER your dog sees your signal.

Avoid HOLDING your signal. Raise your arm, then after the dog starts, lower it. This may tempt her to return without jumping, for which you can correct her. Work with the jumps set wide apart. Work with them close together. Dog show conditions are not always ideal, so practice sessions should not be made easy.

Train your dog to START on signal.

Things To Remember When Teaching The DIRECTED JUMP

Train your dog to START on signal.

When you give the signal, raise your arm by lifting it from your side. If you cross your arm in front of your body before you lift it, your signal contradicts itself.

Hold your signal arm on line with your body, parallel to the ground. Hold the palm of your hand flat, so the dog can see your hand clearly.

When you give the signal, don't **lean** and DON'T move your feet.

While your dog is learning to jump as directed, give praise WITH the signal.

During the first few lessons, keep the jumps low. Make the jumping lesson a game.

Keep the exercise itself simple. After your dog learns to take direction, the test can be made difficult by moving the jumps further apart and raising them to the required full height.

DIRECTED JUMP Problems—How To Overcome Them

Dog Returns Without Jumping

Hold a rolled magazine. Signal the jump, and if your dog comes straight in, wait until she is almost in line with the jumps, then throw the magazine to block her, RUN to the jump you signalled, and encourage her to leap over. The point to keep in mind is not to throw the magazine too soon or your dog will hesitate to jump at all. By checking her in line **with** the hurdles, she will understand the correction was the result of not jumping **as directed.**

Dog Takes Wrong Signal

Same as **Dog Returns Without Jumping,** except the magazine is thrown so that it lands in front, to block the hurdle the dog is taking by mistake. After the correction, run toward the correct hurdle and encourage your dog to come there. Two assistants can help with this exercise—one standing outside the Solid Hurdle, and the other outside the Bar. When the dog heads for the wrong jump, and **is almost there,** the assistant rushes in and blocks her from taking the incorrect hurdle.

Dog Doesn't Start On Signal

If your dog is not the scary type, ask someone to stand behind her while you face her for the DIRECTED JUMP. Signal the jump and follow with a loud "Good Girl!" If the dog doesn't start, the assistant taps the dog's hindquarters with the toe of one shoe. Give extra praise, clap your hands in play, and run toward the jump you signalled.

If the dog is afraid of people, ask the assistant to hide, and when the dog doesn't start on signal, to drop something or make a noise. Give generous praise WITH the correction.

If your dog still doesn't start on signal, take her close to the jump. Ask an assistant to stand alongside the hurdle as when doing the BROAD JUMP in the OPEN CLASS, and to hold the leash, which is fastened to the dog's collar. Face your dog and give the signal to jump. After you give the signal, and while you are giving praise, the assistant jerks the leash forward to make the dog go over. Repeat until the dog jumps on signal from either direction. Follow each signal with praise, whether the leash is jerked or not.

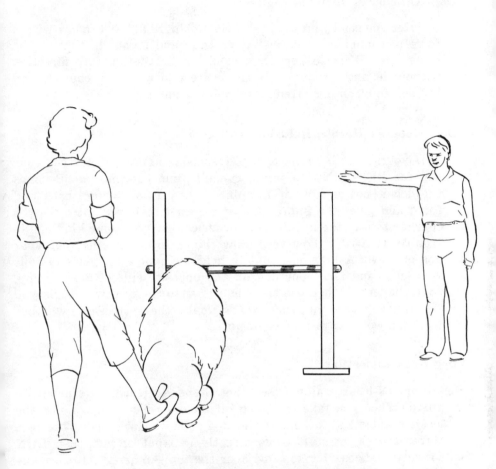

A gentle tap by your assistant will teach your dog to START on signal.

DIRECTED JUMP Problems—How To Overcome Them

Dog Anticipates Jumping Signals

After you send your dog, tell her "Robin, SIT!" and follow with a forceful command "STAY!" Give the hand signal to SIT at the same time. Walk to her, then send her in the opposite direction without letting her jump. If there are assistants, all converge on the dog to block her attempt to jump without permission.

Dog Stops At Hurdle, Refusing To Jump

If your breed is prone to hip dysplasia, before you correct your dog for REFUSING to jump, consult your veterinarian. Perhaps the dog is not capable of jumping. When a dog teeters back and forth and gives the impression of wanting to jump, but lacks the courage to leap the hurdle, the owner can suspect some kind of hip trouble. If X-rays, however, show things to be in order, put your dog on leash. Ask an assistant to hold the handle (or you can do it yourself), and face your dog on the opposite side of a low jump. Give the signal, then use the leash to snap the dog over while you are giving praise. In other words, make the corrections whether your dog would have jumped or not.

Dog Goes Under Bar

For ON-leash training, see **Dog Stops At Hurdle, Refusing To Jump.** When you take the leash off, hold a rolled magazine or the leash wadded into a ball. If the dog tries to duck under the bar, throw the object so it lands directly in front of her, then RUN forward and coax her to come over the top. An assistant can make the correction from the side lines, but here again, timing is important. Blocking should occur just as the head starts under the bar.

So as not to confuse your dog, never use a Bar Jump that has a solid board at the bottom. From the distance, and to small dogs especially, the solid board gives the impression of a Solid Hurdle. When jumping, if your dog then goes **over** the board but **under** the bar, this is not disobedience. You failed to make it clear what you wanted the dog to do.

DIRECTED JUMP Problems—How To Overcome Them

Dog Doesn't Clear Jumps

Providing your dog is free of hip trouble, put her on leash. Ask two assistants to stand, one on each side of the Solid Jump. One assistant holds a light rod along the top board, slightly lower than the board itself. Face your dog on the opposite side of the hurdle and give the command or signal to jump. As your dog goes over, the assistant raises the rod and taps the dog's paws. Give praise with the correction, and don't use the leash except to keep the dog from darting off to the side. The assistant can hold a shorter rod and move it from one side of the hurdle to the other while the dog is jumping. This extends the jump and inadvertently elevates it. The severity with which the correction is made depends upon the size and temperament of the dog. Make the same correction at the Bar Jump.

Dog Is Afraid Of The Bar Jump

Put your dog on leash. Place the bar on the ground between the two uprights. Walk the dog back and forth, giving constant praise. When you raise the bar, do it a little at a time, and step over WITH the dog. When your dog is no longer afraid, and will leap the bar by herself, use the signal without a verbal command. Let the dog decide at what point to take off, so she will gauge the jumping distance and not panic.

DIRECTED JUMPING (COMBINING THE GO AND THE JUMP)

With the jumps set in place and the pulley and line ready for a correction, take your dog to the starting line. Stand **in line with the jumps,** and make your dog sit at heel position. Tell her "Robin, GO!" As she nears the opposite end of the yard, and while she is still moving away, call a cheerful "Robin, SIT! Stay!" If she obeys, say a second "Stay!" and slowly back up to the required distance you must stand when you send your dog in an Obedience Trial. This is approximately twenty feet from the jumps. Signal the Solid Hurdle first (she is more accustomed to this hurdle) by bringing your arm UP from your side. When the arm stops moving, call out a happy "Good Girl!" After she takes direction and is about eight or ten feet from the jump (depending on the size of the dog), call out a forceful "JUMP!" The command, if given at this point, will encourage the dog to go over, in case she is thinking otherwise. Later on, the command is used only as a corrective measure if the dog decides **not** to jump. If your dog doesn't start on signal, you will have to use the jump command along with the arm motion, then give a different jump command for the actual jump. This is permitted in Obedience Trials, but when possible, train your dog to start **without** the jumping command.

If your dog goes out on command for DIRECTED JUMPING, but stops before you tell her, correct her as you did when teaching the DIRECTED GO. Walk to her, snap on the line, tell her "Stay!" then

Combine the GO with the JUMP by starting on the center line.

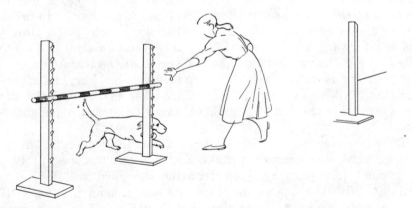

Instead of blocking the dog, run toward the JUMP you signalled.

back away, and, from the distance, call out a second "Go!" Follow by giving the line one hard tug, with praise. Lead her back to the center of the ring, unsnap the line, and try again. If she starts to slow down at the same spot, call out a demanding "GO!" and see if the extra command has the desired effect. If not, repeat the correction until your dog no longer stops without permission.

There are other things your dog may do when you first combine the GO with the JUMP. She may try to jump on the way out. In this case, ask assistants to block her, or call her name sharply. Among other things, she may start for the WRONG jump when signalled, or she may try to come between the jumps on the way back. In either case, RUN to the jump you signalled and pat the top board, or the bar, with the signal hand. If you have two people willing to help, they can run in from the side, but you must move toward the correct jump yourself and encourage your dog to come there. Complete the exercise by having the dog sit in front and, finally, go to the heel position.

Lead your dog forward, not quite to the center of the ring this time, and send her again. When you combine the GO and the JUMP the first few times, the dog is apt to get excited about the jumping, so this part of the exercise should be minimized. By taking the dog forward before you send her, then backing up before she jumps, the hurdles are not so obvious on the GO. With practice, a dog soon learns that she must pass between the hurdles on the GO in order to receive the reward of JUMPING on the way back. Each time you lead her forward, do it less and less, until you can send her successfully between the two hurdles, the full length of the training area.

If your dog is inclined to get "jump happy," send her, and after she is sitting, walk to her, pat her, then send her in the opposite direction. Permitting the dog to jump after every GO, encourages anticipation.

Having perfected the DIRECTED JUMPING exercise in your training yard, buy yourself a stake that you can screw securely into the ground (see page 6). Now transfer the yard training to new locations. With the line set in place and ready, send the dog ONCE, then see what happens. If she stops before you give her the command (most dogs will), make the necessary correction on line, then change the direction of the GO, or move to some other area. The DIRECTED JUMPING ring at dog shows thus becomes just another practice area where she may think you will correct her if she doesn't behave.

Things To Remember When Teaching DIRECTED JUMPING

Have the line and pulley in place, ready for corrections.

Give the first command in a HAPPY tone of voice.

If your dog stops after going a short distance, tell her "Stay!" and snap the line to her collar, then back away, and give the second command WITH the correction. Follow with praise. (See illustration, page 48.)

After your dog does a good GO, call her by name, loudly and cheerfully, to make her turn around, then tell her "Sit!"

Call her name while she is still moving away from you.

Train your dog to start toward the jumps on signal.

Give the signal by lifting your arm from your side.

When you give the signal, don't LEAN, and DON'T move your feet.

After your dog starts, lower your arm, then see if your dog continues toward the jump you signalled.

While your dog is learning to jump as directed, give praise while she is leaping the hurdles.

After your dog knows the exercise, practice in strange surroundings. Make the test difficult! Send your dog under trying conditions. Make her jump hurdles she is not familiar with, or hurdles set ridiculously close together or extremely far apart.

GROUP EXAMINATION

The problems normally encountered in the GROUP EXAMINA-
TION are those of the STAND FOR EXAMINATION and the SIT-
and DOWN-stays of the Novice and Open Classes. One exception is
the dog with a bad temper that will be under control when his handler
stands at the end of the leash, but who can't be trusted with the
handler some distance away. Except for this one problem, the GROUP
EXAMINATION should be easier than the STAND FOR EXAMI-
NATION of the Novice Class. The majority of problems will already
have been overcome and it is mostly a matter of training the dog to
stand for a longer period of time, and to take examination from
strangers while the owner stands at a distance.

But easy or not, the GROUP EXAMINATION should be practiced
in unfamiliar surroundings. Dogs expect to be corrected on home
ground or in the training yard. By creating a situation in which the
dog thinks she doesn't have to be obedient, effective corrections can
be made that will carry over into the Obedience ring. Even a trained
dog will take advantage if she thinks she can get away with it!

Things To Remember When Teaching GROUP EXAMINATION

Leave your dog in a comfortable position with feet placed naturally.

When you put your arm band and leash on the ground, place them far enough away that your dog won't be tempted to sniff them.

Give the signal and command to stay **before** you move your feet.

When you walk away, step off on your RIGHT foot, and leave from an upright position. Crouching may cause your dog to lie down or to follow.

While away from your dog, don't fidget.

Train the dog to stand from six to eight minutes. The three-minute stand will then seem short in comparison.

When you return to your dog, circle slowly.

When the exercise is finished, pat the dog while she is still in a standing position.

Dog Sits During The Three-Minute Test

Accustom your dog to long periods of standing. During training, wrap the leash loosely around your dog's stomach before you leave her. The surcingle will be most effective if you used the leash to teach the stand.

Alternate correction: If your dog sits during practice, fasten a twenty-five- to thirty-foot line to the dog's collar, and **pull** her to a standing position from the distance. Command her to "Stand! Stay!" in a voice of authority.

When you take the leash off, surreptitiously place something underneath your dog—a toy or some object that will jump or make a squawking noise when she sits on it. With some dogs, this will be effective. Other dogs will not be impressed. Certain types will play with the article!

One method of teaching your dog to STAND for a long period of time.

GROUP EXAMINATION Problems—How To Overcome Them

Dog Is Overly Friendly With The Judge

Ask those who examine your dog during practice to hold the back of one hand toward the dog's muzzle as they approach her. When the dog moves forward to greet them, ask them to cuff the dog's nose with the back of their hand and at the same time, to stroke the dog with the other hand.

Dog Sniffs The Ground While Standing

Every time your dog lowers her head, call out a loud "HI!" or "Pay attention!" If the sniffing continues, toss something at the spot the dog is sniffing, or squirt some water at her.

Dog Shies From Judge

When you face your dog, hold something you can throw from a distance. When your dog shies from the person who is examining her, throw what you are holding so it lands in front of the dog, in whichever direction she moves. At the same time, call out loudly, "STAY!" The person examining praises and reassures the dog while stroking her.

Dog Growls During Examination

Same as **Dog Shies From Judge,** but more forcefully.

Another suggestion to overcome these two problems is to ask four or five people to circle your dog, all at the same time. This is done, first, without touching the dog, then gradually each person, in turn, strokes the dog reassuringly and gives praise. Being surrounded on all sides, and fearing to move in any one direction, your dog may overcome her fear of people, the cause of her shying away or growling at the judge.

Dog Goes To Another Dog

Teach your dog to stay away from other dogs. During practice, give your friends who have dogs with them, magazines to hold. When your dog runs to sniff theirs, ask them to cuff your dog on the nose with the magazine. If they are not holding a magazine, they should use the back of their hand instead.

GROUP EXAMINATION Problems—How To Overcome Them

If your dog is a fighter and isn't to be trusted, muzzle her with a length of 2" gauze bandage. Make a loop in the center, slip it over the dog's nose and pull it tight. Bring both ends upward under the ears and make a bowknot on top of the neck. Association with other dogs while muzzled, may help your dog get over her scrappiness.

Dog Moves Forward On Stand

Before you leave your dog to stand at a distance, quietly snap the leash to her collar, fastening the handle end to a stationary object in back of the dog. If you prefer, a friend can hold the leash (or a long line), looped around the dog's stomach. When the dog creeps forward, the owner calls out a demanding "Stay!" and the assistant pulls the dog back.

Dog Sits When Handler Returns

During practice, return to heel position; wait, then leave your dog again. Do this as many times as necessary until your dog will remain standing until you give her permission to move.

SUGGESTIONS FOR EXHIBITING IN THE UTILITY
OBEDIENCE CLASSES AT DOG SHOWS

There are probably more failures in the Utility Classes than in any other classes in Obedience Trials. For this reason owners should prepare their dogs for the unexpected before ENTERING a trial. Train your dog in strange locations and under trying conditions. It is the FIRST correction in new surroundings that makes an impression during the training. This is especially true of the DIRECTED JUMPING. If you wish to carry the "perfect" performance of the training yard into the Obedience ring, move to a new location each time you practice and your dog will be more dependable at dog shows.

Read the Obedience "rule book"* carefully and familiarize yourself with the show ring procedure. The extra commands and signals, and body gestures you used to train your dog, are not permitted in a regular trial.

By the time your dog is ready for the UTILITY Class, if you have been doing the exhibiting yourself, you are no longer an amateur when it comes to dog shows. Take the usual precautions of watering and exercising your dog; of leaving the uninterested worker alone a few minutes prior to working; of observing the ring procedure that day (unless your dog is the first to work); but more important, be careful how you handle your dog. In the UTILITY Class more than anywhere else, HANDLING plays an important part.

---

* **Regulations and Standards for Obedience Trials** available from: The American Kennel Club, 51 Madison Ave., New York, N.Y. 10010. The Canadian Kennel Club, 667 Yonge St., Toronto, Canada. Obedience rules are revised occasionally. Make certain you have the latest copy.

For the SCENT DISCRIMINATION exercise, let your dog sit quietly at heel position, without distracting her, and let her see the scent articles go down. Knowing where the unscented articles are placed may make the difference between success and failure.

For the SIGNAL EXERCISE, keep your signals distinct. Hold your arm away from your body and wear clothing that doesn't blend into the landscape. If you trained your dog to obey without resorting to extreme body motions (the ideal way of training), remember that the slightest motion on your part may be the signal your dog is waiting for. Nervous or not, don't fidget! Most of all, refrain from giving a signal when your dog is looking away. If she doesn't see the signal, she should hardly be failed for refusing to take the signal.

The DIRECTED JUMPING exercise requires precaution of equal importance. CLEAR signals BEFORE the jumping command are essential.

For the final test, the GROUP EXAMINATION, leave your dog standing comfortably in a natural position.

Even a trained dog is easily distracted, so a heavier tone of voice (no yelling) may be the answer if your dog is thinking of other things than obedience.

If your dog is "ringwise," and takes advantage when she knows she can get away with it, sanctioned matches allow you to make correction, which you can't make in a regular Obedience Trial.

When a dog is consistently ringwise, try changing handlers. A strange voice of authority may get your dog over the hump.

If your dog has failed one or two trials because she didn't START an exercise, perhaps it is your command! The S sound of the "Sit!" or "Stay!" used to correct anticipation, is similar to "Seek!" if you use this command for SCENT DISCRIMINATION. Change commands!

When trying for your dog's UTILITY degree, don't be tempted to enter her in the OPEN Class at the same trial. Two different classes may confuse your dog until she has had more experience.

Be proud of your UTILITY trained dog. Make her a credit to Obedience.

TRACKING

TRACKING looks hard and it IS hard, but like the other Obedience exercises, when taken step by step, teaching a dog to track is not an impossibility, not even for the amateur. TRACKING takes more TIME than the other Obedience exercises, as well as more SPACE. And learning to "read" your dog is an art at which not everyone is proficient; but the satisfaction in being able to put the letter T after your dog's U.D. Obedience degree, makes every TRACKING ordeal worthwhile.

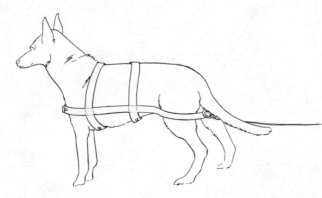

A tracking harness that doesn't hinder the dog's freedom of action. The line used for the DIRECTED GO can be used as a tracking line.

FACTORS THAT WILL INFLUENCE YOUR DOG'S ABILITY TO TRACK

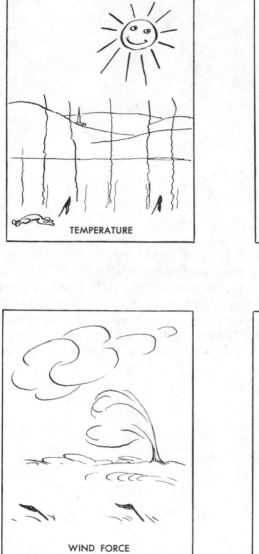

TEMPERATURE

ATMOSPHERIC CONDITIONS

WIND FORCE

TYPE OF TERRAIN

The Why And Wherefore Of Tracking

The human body constantly sheds scale-like particles, the odor of which permeates the air around the body and the ground over which a person walks. Like fingerprints, everyone has his own variety of "odor," which makes it possible for dogs, noted for their keen sense of smell, to distinguish between scents—a skill called TRACKING or TRAILING. When a dog fails to perform adequately in a regulation Tracking Test, more often than not it is the human element, a part of every test, or the rules themselves that are to blame. One drawback is the fact that the dogs are restricted by a tracking line. This limits their freedom to cover ground. Tracking being a subject not too many people are familiar with, the dogs are interfered with by incompetent handling and handicapped by improperly laid tracks. And, very often, the judges are at fault because they expect too much of a dog, insisting upon a precision-like performance.

In spite of unfortunate tracking conditions now and then, owners with little knowledge and NO experience have ventured forth on their own to train their dog sufficiently well to pass an official tracking test. Some have had the "luck of the Irish" and have got their dogs through on the first attempt, after two or three weeks of training. Others have tried for years without success. The AVERAGE owner faces months of hard work, and at least one or two tracking test failures, before he can heave a sighing "We made it!" and mentally make plans to frame the coveted TRACKING certificate.

The amateur, when he attempts to teach his dog TRACKING, should remember certain facts about nose work on which experienced handlers agree. For one thing, scent is more pronounced after sundown, when atmospheric conditions cause odors to cling more closely to the ground, and in the early morning as the ground scent starts to rise. A cloudy day with heavy weather is preferable, when teaching, to one that is hot, dry, and windy. Wind enhances the dog's scenting ability under certain conditions, but it changes the tracking act to one of trailing.

Moving objects, such as running water or shifting leaves, break the line of scent, which must be recovered on stationary objects, while strong odors (tar or gasoline for instance) keep every dog from doing the best scent work. It is also agreed that breeds of dogs and dogs within a breed vary in their ability to use their noses.

TRACKING EQUIPMENT

Tracking equipment consists of a harness, a tracking line, articles to be dropped, and five or six stakes tied with a small piece of colored material. The stakes can be made of metal or wood, and the length of them is determined by the type of ground over which the dog tracks, but their color should blend into the landscape. Dogs are quick to follow an obviously marked path.

The twenty- to sixty-foot tracking line, made of webbing, nylon or ordinary clothesline, should have a snap at one end and a looped handle or a knot at the other end. The harness can be any type, but one similar to that shown in the illustration on page 71 is practical, and will get your dog off to a good start. This harness acts as a set of traces like those used to pull a wagon, and the dog is free to pivot to the right or to the left, or to circle completely, without becoming entangled in the tracking line.

If the training collar is used instead of a harness, the line must be attached in such a way that the collar won't tighten when the dog pulls ahead.

Later, include among tracking equipment, a policeman's whistle, a notebook, a pencil, a timepiece, a compass, and a pair of binoculars, if you have one. In hot weather, carry a jug of water for yourself as well as the dog.

And, speaking of equipment, when you finish tracking for the day, the easy method of rolling the line by holding it between the thumb and index finger and folding it over the elbow, is taboo. You'll spend hours the next time you practice, untangling it. Instead, gather the line up by hooking it first on one thumb and then on the other. This folds the line in layers, a pattern that is less likely to become twisted or entangled.

TRACKING THE OWNER'S SCENT

Teaching a dog to use her nose for a specific purpose is the basic principle of TRACKING. Lessons will be made easier if you play games with your dog, even as a puppy, requiring her to hunt for hidden objects. These games can be started in the house during an evening or on a rainy day, then transferred to the outdoors. Later, try sending your dog for "lost" articles after dark so she will **have to** use her nose to find them.

Another method of teaching your dog to sniff the ground, or the air, is to have someone hold your dog while YOU disappear. Since you are the dog's favorite person, when told to "Find!" she should take off immediately, using eyes, nose, or both, to discover where you went. Transfer this training to a second person, selecting someone the dog is especially fond of. This playful tracking in the form of a game conditions your dog for more serious lessons which follow.

Prior to field training, exercise your dog and give her a drink of water. Such things may seem unimportant, but your dog will be more interested in her work if she has physical comfort. Now teach her, through a series of retrieves in long grass with tracking line attached to the harness and DRAGGING, that the backward pull on the line is NOT a correction. Get her interest and let her SEE you throw the article (leather glove or wallet) some distance away. Tell her "Find!" and encourage her to go for the article immediately. The tightening of the line may at first cause concern. To the Obedience trained dog, TRACKING will be a new experience. It may even come as a shock when you encourage her to lead the way on line instead of reprimanding her for not staying at heel position, but she must now learn to pull ahead.

Assuming that the dog has overcome all fear of the tracking line and will advance to its full length, and providing she will seek a lost article in long grass and bring it back to you, it is time to plot a single straight track. And, as tracking fields in some parts of the country are at a premium, TAKE CARE HOW YOU HANDLE THE PLOTTED AREA and you will be able to use the same track over and over again.

Select an open field—one, if possible, where you can head into the wind, and with knee-length grass, which holds scent better than a golf course or a well-kept lawn. Tie your dog or tell her "Stay!" Then place your starting stake, walk around it several times, head INTO the wind, walk thirty to forty paces, place a second stake and return over the same path. Wear leather-soled shoes in preference to rubber footwear, to give your dog every advantage. Rubber has a strong odor that could interfere with your dog's first attempts to follow human scent. Later, it won't make any difference, except in an official Tracking Test, WHAT the tracklayer wears, but the preliminary lessons should be as easy as possible.

With your dog sitting at heel position, let her SEE you throw one of the articles as far as you can on the direct line of the track. If she darts off, line dragging, be generous with your praise, especially when she finds the article. If she hesitates to go for it, walk slowly along the track with her until she finds it, then return to the starting stake by walking back over the SAME track. You are trying to economize—remember?

Leaving your dog at the starting stake, walk the track again and let her SEE YOU DROP the article close to the second stake. Return, give the command "Find!" and see if she will dash for it immediately. If successful in this exercise, leave her at the starting stake and, this time, walk to the second stake and, taking the stake with you, INCREASE THE DISTANCE by another twenty-five to thirty paces. Place the stake; let the dog SEE you drop the article; return; send her and see if she will go the greater distance. If she acts uncertain, give encouragement! If she dashes for the article, give praise!

Each time the dog runs the track, the lessons should be made more difficult. Now walk the track and drop the article at the second stake WITHOUT the dog's seeing you drop it. Return, send her, and if she successfully finds the article, it is time to make a single turn, or to angle off in another direction. Carry a third stake when you walk the track this time, and make an approximately 90-degree turn at the second stake. Proceed another thirty paces, place the third stake, and drop your article. After you drop it, walk back to the second stake, turn, then head for the starting stake. Before you tell your dog "Find," be sure the tracking line is not tangled, and plan to go with your dog. The best method of handling the line is to spread it out in a zigzag pattern over the ground, and when the dog starts, to let the line slide through your LEFT hand until you feel the handle. By allowing your dog to pull out to almost the full length of the line BEFORE YOU MOVE, motion behind the dog won't distract her. When you move, be as quiet as possible.

As your dog approaches the turn, observe wind direction. If the first leg of the track was laid INTO the wind, the dog will probably turn BEFORE she reaches the stake. If it was laid WITH the wind, she may go past it before she turns. The dog will indicate the turn by circling. When she does, STAND STILL! Wait until she starts forward on the second leg of the track, then follow cautiously, giving gentle praise. When she reaches the article, show extra enthusiasm, but DON'T MESS UP THE TRACK. After your dog retrieves the article, keep her at heel position and REWALK the track by returning to the second stake, turning, and going back to the starting stake.

Your dog may, by now, try to "run" the track like a fifty-yard dash. A dog should work quickly, but not so fast as to overshoot turns. The fact that the dog is restricted by the line and can't backtrack to recapture a lost scent means she may lose the scent entirely. If you have a fast-working dog, keep the line taut (as when driving a horse), walk quickly or move at a slow "dog trot," but don't RUN. When the dog stops and begins to circle, STAND STILL! Wait for her to make the next move, in case she wants to retrace her steps. If your dog is a slow, deliberate performer, she will probably not move faster than a walk at any time, so all you will have to do in this case is to hold the handle of the line, follow when the dog moves, and stop when she stops.

Your next step in teaching your dog to track will be to increase the length of the SECOND leg. Walk the track again and again, moving stake #3 further out each time. Finally, carry a fourth stake, and turn at stake #3, making a third leg of the track. When your dog shows proficiency on two turns, try three or more. Try dropping more than one article at spaced intervals BETWEEN the stakes. Each time you do the exercise, KEEP REWALKING THE TRACK. Just as the Obedience trained dog, after several attempts at an exercise, will do the exercise more easily, the TRACKING dog learns more quickly what is expected of her when given reruns over the SAME track,

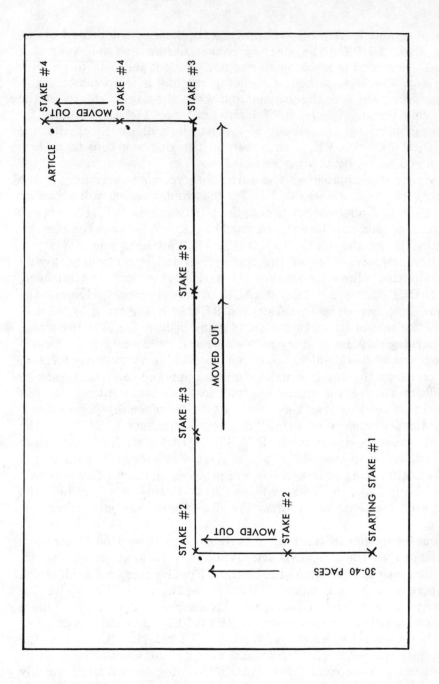

TEACHING TRACKING BY REWALKING THE TRACK

78

which by this time is well scented with human odor and well marked by broken twigs and grasses, and by disturbed dirt and stones.

The manner in which your dog "takes the scent" is not too important up to this point. So far, TRACKING has been treated as a SEEK BACK exercise, with the dog very much aware of which scent to follow. If she wanders around the starting stake, sniffs the ground in various places, then takes off on her own, this is the ideal way of starting. But, during a tracking test, consider the combination of human scents! On the day prior to the test, three people (and probably more) will have trampled the fields while plotting the tracks, the greatest part of the trampling taking place in the area of the starting stakes. Although one person will rewalk the track the following morning, the mixture of human scents will not yet have been expended by the time your dog begins to work. Your responsibility as a handler is to help your dog get started on the **right** scent.

If the dogs could be given an article belonging to the tracklayer to sniff at the starting stake, owners wouldn't have to be so cautious about the start. The article would **identify** the scent. But since we can't tell the dog in so many words WHOSE scent to follow, we must do what we can to help the dog start on the correct one. Train your dog to lie down or to sit quietly, close to the starting stake, while you untangle the tracking line and spread it over the ground. This will give the dog time to concentrate on the more RECENT scent in case other human scents are in the area. To track a **special** person, your dog must have that person's scent at the start of the track.

Things To Remember When Teaching
TRACKING THE OWNER'S SCENT

Use the proper equipment.

Exercise and water your dog BEFORE training. In hot weather take a jug of water to the field with you.

Start with retrieves in long grass, with tracking line dragging.

When you plot the first track, place stake #1 in an open field, circle it several times, walk a single track into the wind, place stake #2, then return to the starting stake.

Do a series of retrieves on direct line of the track.

Walk the track and let the dog SEE you place the article. Do this several times.

Walk the track and drop the article WITHOUT the dog's seeing it fall.

Lengthen the single track by moving stake #2 OUTWARD.

When your dog is reliable on a straight track, introduce a turn. Remember to REWALK the track.

After you give the command, let your dog pull out to the full length of the line BEFORE you follow.

Give gentle encouragement but avoid distracting your dog by unnecessary talking or excessive waving of your arms.

Your dog will not always follow where you walked.

Observe wind direction.

Never permit your dog to puddle (or your male to lift his leg) without a correction. No tracking dog should be distracted.

Interesting smells; idle curiosity about other animals or objects; or lack of interest at the start, require a definite command of "FIND!" given in a voice of authority.

While working, if your dog stops or circles back toward you, STAND STILL! When she moves on, follow quietly.

Be generous with praise when the dog finds the article.

Unless you have finished tracking for the day, return to the starting stake by REWALKING the track so you can use the track again.

If your dog simply refuses to follow a track, go back to the beginning and review tracking procedure, step by step.

If your dog won't pick up the article from long grass, see **RETRIEVE ON FLAT Problems—How To Overcome Them,** in **The Complete Open Obedience Course.**

Train for endurance, not for speed! A fast moving dog may last the 440 to 500 yards required in a Tracking Test, but how would she stand up on a full day's run?

TRACKING A STRANGER'S SCENT

Having taught your dog basic tracking on your own scent, it is time to introduce the scent of a second person. Move to a fresh field, or to one where you have not worked for a few days, and start with a short straight track. It is a loss of time and a waste of tracking fields to have a second person lay a full-length track until you know your dog will follow a simple track belonging to a stranger. Substituting the scent of the second person for your own, review tracking lessons from the beginning. Ask person #2 to throw the seek back article in tall grass, then YOU give the command "Find!" Have person #2 walk a track into the wind, return, then throw the article on direct line of the track, just as you did. Have person #2 walk the same track and let the dog SEE the placing of the article on the ground. After the tracklayer returns and the dog retrieves the dropped article, have person #2 drop the article WITHOUT the dog's seeing it fall.

How long should you work? That's hard to say. It depends on the dog, on the kind of day it is, and the amount of progress you make. A good "stopping point" is to have the lesson end on a happy note, your dog having accomplished something new that day.

When teaching your dog to follow the scent of a stranger, do so by stages. Have the tracklayer first increase the length of the single track, then later introduce a single turn. Remind the tracklayer, though, to walk the track both going and COMING, so the track can be used over again. After lengthening the second leg, the tracklayer should make a second turn, gradually working up to a full-length track with several turns.

The tracklayer's role is an important one. Poor judgment when plotting the course, both in practice and at a Tracking Test, has caused many dogs to fail. The good tracklayer judges the situation, not through the **eyes** of the human, but through the **nose** of the dog.

Things The Tracklayer Should Remember When Plotting A Track

Scent will blow 75 to 150 feet—even further! Stay away from boundary lines and water, and avoid tricky field openings.

When possible, avoid having parallel legs of a track close together.

Avoid bushes and small trees, which tend to pocket scent.

Keep all turns a 90-degree angle or more.

Keep the track simple. Wind plays enough tricks as it is.

In a cross wind, the scent will blow to your right or to your left.

If the wind is in your face when you make a turn, the dog will turn before YOU do. If the wind is at your back, she will turn AFTER you make the turn. Make allowances for wind direction.

If you walk along a ditch, your scent may be IN the ditch.

If you walk over a hill, your scent will SURROUND the hill.

Avoid dropping the article on hilly terrain, directly AFTER a turn. Scent on a high point spreads out as it seeks a lower level. The article could be overlooked, the dog following, instead, where you left the field. Even if you return by rewalking the track, the dog could be confused by the widely scented area.

After dropping the article (unless the track is being rewalked), continue at least fifty paces, preferably more, BEFORE TURNING.

Human scent is stronger than scent left on an article, so while the dog is working, remain DOWN WIND and stay away from the dog at the start.

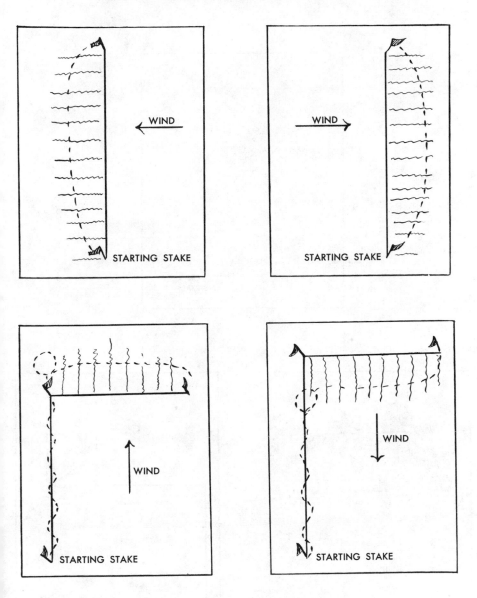

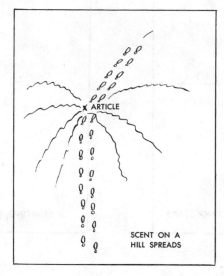

SCENT ON A
HILL SPREADS

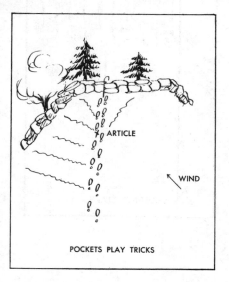

POCKETS PLAY TRICKS

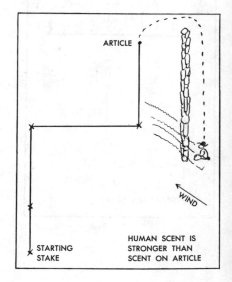

HUMAN SCENT IS
STRONGER THAN
SCENT ON ARTICLE

Up until now, the stakes have been left in the ground to allow the trainer to use the same field over and over again, and to check the dog for accuracy. But the stakes have got to go sooner or later, so it might as well be now. If you lay the track yourself, place the starting stake, then a second stake thirty yards out. This is to get your dog accustomed to seeing two stakes close together, the same set-up used in a regulation tracking test. Continue forty to fifty paces past the second stake, place a third stake, turn, continue walking another forty to fifty paces, and place another stake to mark the second turn; walk the third leg, place stake #5, and drop the article. Then REWALK the track, picking up the two stakes at the turns. For now, stake #5 is left in the ground in case the dog fails to find the dropped article. It is no fun hunting for the article yourself! If someone else lays the track for you, have the tracklayer do the same, picking up all stakes on the return trip EXCEPT the stake where the article was dropped, the starting stake, and the stake thirty yards from the start. The "pattern" of your dog's track, without the stakes to guide her, will soon tell you if your dog is using her nose or whether she has been putting one over on you and "cheating" because she was stake-wise.

It is time now for the tracks to "cool." After the track has been laid, let your dog wait ten minutes before starting. Let her wait twenty! Let her wait even longer! Your dog may have to wait as long as two hours in a Tracking Test. Keeping the dog waiting isn't the hardship you think. Dogs distrust changes. They like to acclimate themselves to such things as new terrain, wind directions, people, and other animals, before concentrating on scent work. Don't rush your dog and she will do better work. While waiting, take advantage of the "wait." Lay a second track that can be cooling while your dog is working the first track.

Now that your dog KNOWS how to follow a track, it is time for YOU to place more confidence in your dog. From now on, you must no longer know in which direction the track lies. Through a pre-arranged whistling code, the tracklayer can inform you from a distance if you are completely off course, or if you are interfering with the dog in any way. Until your dog is dependable, have the tracklayer leave a stake where the article was dropped. This will help in a glorious finish. When this stake is also removed, ask the tracklayer to select some marker (a tree or a pole) that will guide him in case your dog fails to find the article. Tracking articles are elusive creatures!

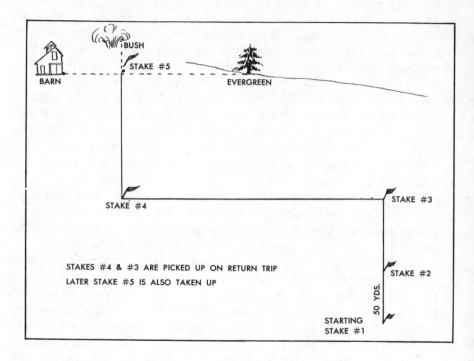

From this point on, work up gradually to a full-length track that meets the specifications for a Tracking Test. Introduce all conditions under which your dog will be required to work. The actual distance is approximately a quarter of a mile long and the scent, which is that of a stranger, is from half an hour to two hours old. There are at least two turns in the open fields; and the tracks at no time follow a natural boundary closer than ten yards. For complete instructions, see The American or Canadian Kennel Club rule book, **Regulations and Standards for Obedience Trials.**

Things To Remember When Teaching
TRACKING A STRANGER'S SCENT

During the learning stage, ask that the fields be plotted to the best advantage. Keep tracks short and uncomplicated.

See that the tracklayer is wearing leather-soled shoes (later, except in a test, let him wear anything).

Have the ground well scuffed-up at the start, and request the "tracklayer's shuffle" (dragging the feet).

Ask that all turns be made well in the open, and that the track not be laid close to a natural boundary line.

Observe the tracklayer when he drops the article. See that he continues in a straight line for quite some distance before making a turn. If you are not watching the laying of the track, ask the tracklayer to assume this responsibility.

Insist that the tracklayer remain DOWN wind while the dog is working. If the track is rewalked, have the tracklayer stay away from the start.

Be sure your dog is rested, has had water, and is properly exercised before working.

Let your dog remain close to the starting stake while you stretch the line to its full length. This will give your dog time to concentrate on the scent.

Give the command "Find!" or "Seek!" calmly, without being too demanding.

BEFORE you give the command, observe the wind direction. This will tell whether your dog should work on line with the stakes, or off to one side or the other.

After you give the command, STAND STILL. Let your dog pull out almost to the full length of the line before you start walking.

Avoid winding the tracking line into a ball. If you must take up slack while your dog is working, slide the line through your hands and play it out in back of you.

Avoid talking to your dog unnecessarily or calling her name.

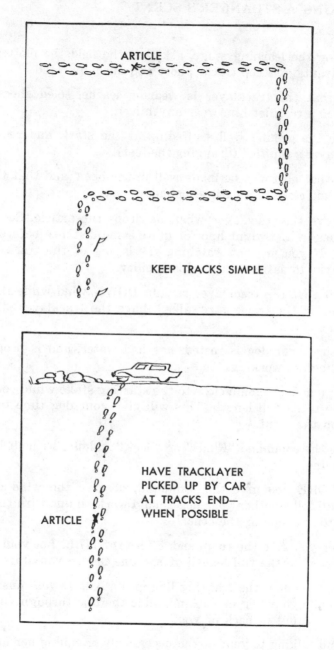

KEEP TRACKS SIMPLE

HAVE TRACKLAYER
PICKED UP BY CAR
AT TRACKS END—
WHEN POSSIBLE

88

If your dog appears to be scenting, a quiet "Good Girl!" is all the encouragement she needs.

Avoid jerking the line as your dog advances. Don't let her think she is being corrected.

Walk quickly! Dog trot! Don't see how fast you can run!

When your dog begins to circle, STAND STILL! Wait for her to take her next direction before you continue forward.

If your dog stops to do things she shouldn't, snap the line sharply and in a demanding tone say "GO FIND!" When a dog is distracted by little things, she is not thinking of her work.

Praise generously when your dog finds the article.

Review lessons whenever your dog appears confused. Start from the beginning.

As the weeks roll by, and you and your dog continue TRACK-ING, practice early in the morning. Practice late at night. Track in bright sun and on a rainy day. Owners will find that an old track on a rainy day is less broad than on a hot sunny day, making it easier to follow.

Track in wind, and over all types of terrain. Introduce a cross track. Have a second person walk across the regular track and when you come to the "fork," see which direction your dog takes. If your dog follows the original track and ignores the cross track, you have little to worry about.

As in other Obedience exercises, when you hit a snag, go back to basic training. Keep tracks short to make the lessons more interesting. If it is practice on starts you need, do only starts on single, straight tracks. If your dog is weak on turns, a series of turns on a zigzag course may give your dog the confidence she needs.

Most of all, learn to "read" your dog. If a dog wanders off disinterestedly, glancing from side to side with an occasional look over her shoulder to see what you are doing, she is merely going for a walk. Return to the starting stake and give her another try. If she darts off in a businesslike manner, head down, tail wagging (if she has a tail), crossing and recrossing the direct line of track, the dog knows pretty much what she is looking for. Follow without distracting her.

WHILE TRACKING AVOID

NATURAL
BOUNDARIES

TRICKY
OPENINGS

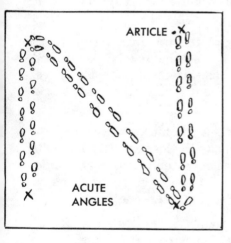

ARTICLE

ACUTE
ANGLES

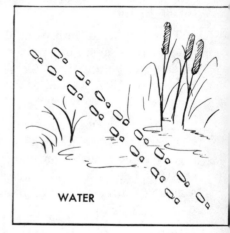

WATER

Circling indicates uncertainty. This may also be a sign the track turns in another direction. For this reason, it is important that you STAND STILL when your dog begins to circle. If you urge her on, the tracking line may not be sufficiently long for her to find the turn she missed.

Lifting the head and sniffing the air frequently means the dog has lost the ground scent, which she is trying to recapture as airborne scent. Under these conditions, give the dog as much freedom as you can. An increase of speed means the dog is hot on the trail, and close to her objective. Tight circles ending in a stalking attitude indicate the end of the trail, and the object she seeks.

Unless your dog is exceptionally fast, test your **handling** ability. Let the tracking line drag while your dog runs the track. Watch the line closely. When the line stops, you stop! When it moves on again, move along with it. This will keep you from interfering with your dog if she HAPPENS to be right when you THINK the track goes in another direction. Have you ever tracked in snow? You will be surprised at the things you will learn about TRACKING that you never knew before!

TRACKING Problems—How To Overcome Them

Dog Appears To Be Tracking, With No Results

Learn to read your dog more carefully. Watch for these SIGNS: **Quick pivots** as the dog double checks the scent, both at ground level and in the air. **Concentration!** If your dog is working, she will be unmindful of what is happening around her. Note **head carriage** and **tail wag** (if she has a tail). Head and tail carriage point out quite definitely whether your dog is working or out for a good time.

Dog Shows Disinterest

Review tracking lessons from the beginning and if your dog still indicates lack of interest, try giving the starting command in a demanding tone of voice.

Dog Starts, Then Gets Discouraged

Perhaps you unconsciously interfere with your dog while she is working. If your dog knows how to track, have confidence in her tracking ability. Don't pull her off the scent just because YOU think the track goes in another direction. Don't plan in your mind how a field will have been plotted; and when your dog is working, avoid jerking the line so she won't think the pull on her harness is a correction.

Dog Gets Bored, Then Just Stands

If your dog knows TRACKING and is merely trying to get out of work, and IF YOU DEFINITELY KNOW WHERE THE TRACK GOES, take the ring of her collar, and give a series of hard jerks along the track, using a demanding "FIND!" When the dog starts working the track again, follow with encouraging praise.

Dog Uses Eyes To Find Article Instead Of Scenting With Nose

Run tracks after dark. Practice retrieves and the Seek Back exercise where there is little light.

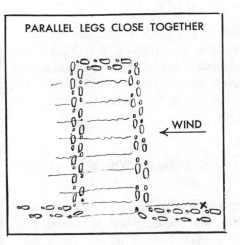

PARALLEL LEGS CLOSE TOGETHER

WIND

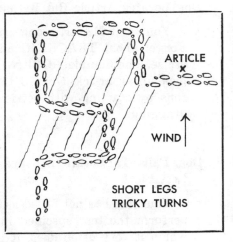

ARTICLE

WIND

SHORT LEGS
TRICKY TURNS

• ARTICLE

DROPPING ARTICLE
ON HILL AFTER A TURN

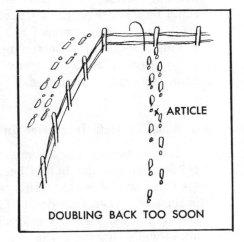

ARTICLE

DOUBLING BACK TOO SOON

TRACKING Problems—How To Overcome Them

Dog Locates Article But Refuses To Pick It Up

You can't MAKE a dog track but you CAN make her retrieve. Forget about TRACKING and review RETRIEVE ON FLAT exercise, **The Complete OPEN Obedience Course.** When your dog will pick up .an article ON COMMAND, review basic TRACKING lessons by starting with retrieves in long grass, with tracking line dragging.

Dog Fails To Locate Dropped Article—Follows Where Tracklayer Left Field

Your dog has not failed as a tracking dog. She has only failed to perform the test specified in the rule book. When this happens, which it very often does, it is just hard luck. This situation may be avoided by having the tracklayer refrain from dropping the article directly after a turn; by having the tracklayer continue in a straight line fifty paces or more, after dropping the article, before turning; or by having the tracklayer picked up by car to prevent circling back, close to the original track. This situation could be PREVENTED by having the tracklayer backtrack on the trail, so the scent would END where the article is dropped, or by having the dog find a person, not an article. Still another way would be to use a helicopter and have the tracklayer lifted from the field after the article is dropped.

Dog Wets, Or Gets Interested In Other Things While Working

This is usually due to carelessness during training. One doesn't think much of a dog in an Obedience Trial that goes to the ringside, visiting; or a dog that deliberately wets when told to retrieve. It is the same when your dog is TRACKING. If you exercise your dog before you ask her to work, she shouldn't have to relieve herself again while running a short track. Use the line and throw the dog off balance when she starts to sit down, or when the male dog lifts his leg. If animals and birds are what's interesting, use a more demanding command, "FIND!"

TRACKING Problems—How To Overcome Them

Dog Won't Start

Work on **starts**. Review retrieve lessons on direct line of a single track until your dog will go out on the first command to get the thrown article. Graduate to PLACING the article on the track. When you send your dog for an article she did not see dropped, use demanding commands of "Find! Find! Find!" and when she starts, let the dog pull out to almost the full length of the line before you follow.

If your dog still refuses to start for an object on command, review SCENT DISCRIMINATION and DIRECTED RETRIEVE Problems—How To Overcome Them.

Dog Appears Confused About Correct Scent

Practice in the early morning before ground scent starts to rise. Practice after sundown when atmospheric conditions hold scent close to the ground. During practice sessions, let your dog sniff some article near the starting stake, belonging to the tracklayer. Carry the article in a bag and give the dog another sniff occasionally, to remind her of the scent she is looking for. Ask the tracklayer to drop a series of articles and after your dog finds them, let her find the person who dropped them.

Dog Misses Turns

Is your dog tracking too fast? Slow her down; and remember, STOP when she stops. Practice turns. Plot a zigzag course, leaving stakes at each turn, and observe how your dog works the turns. Perhaps you are to blame because you interfere!

MORE ADVANCED TRACKING

The grueling test required of dogs in police work may never become a part of The American Kennel Club and Canadian Kennel Club rules, but it is always a challenge to teach one's pet dog this more intricate phase of TRACKING.

When your dog is capable of following the type of track for which she would be awarded the Kennel Club TRACKING certificate, and if you have already tested your dog on a single cross track, have two cross tracks laid by TWO different people. Test your dog even further by having another dog or some other animal cross the track, even doubling back on the original track. Regardless of extra tracks, your dog should stay with the one on which she started.

Give your dog the water test. Select a small stream and ask the tracklayer, when he enters the stream, to walk upstream or downstream twenty-five to thirty paces before exiting on the other side. When your dog indicates loss of scent at the edge of the stream, take her across the stream and see if she can pick the scent up there.

Use a six-foot leash and work your dog through underbrush, over stone walls, and through openings a person would normally use when going for a walk. Cross heavily traveled roads, and after your dog finds one or two clues on a track, let her find the person responsible for the clues. Experiment with tracks that have cooled, leaving them for twelve hours or longer.

It will be a thrilling moment when your dog is capable of recapturing scent in a new location, both tracklayer and dog having been transported to the unfamiliar area by car or other means of transportation. Perhaps someday our T.D.'s. will be given a higher rating for which they will be certified as qualified trackers, available to authorities for use in missing person searches. In the meantime, the sport of Advanced TRACKING remains an enjoyable, exciting hobby. The exercise is stimulating; the outdoor life exhilarating; and there is always the practical side of owning a well-trained TRACKING dog.